MySQL® Clustering

Alex Davies and Harrison Fisk

MySQL Press

800 East 96th Street, Indianapolis, Indiana 46240 USA

MySQL Clustering

International Standard Book Number: 0-672-32855-0

Library of Congress Catalog Card Number: 2005931176

Printed in the United States of America

First Printing: March 2006

09 08 07 06   4 3 2 1

Trademarks

All terms mentioned in this book that are known to be trademarks or service marks have been appropriately capitalized. Pearson Education cannot attest to the accuracy of this information. Use of a term in this book should not be regarded as affecting the validity of any trademark or service mark.

Warning and Disclaimer

Every effort has been made to make this book as complete and as accurate as possible, but no warranty or fitness is implied. The information provided is on an "as is" basis. The authors and the publisher shall have neither liability nor responsibility to any person or entity with respect to any loss or damages arising from the information contained in this book.

Bulk and Special Sales

Pearson offers excellent discounts on this book when ordered in quantity for bulk purchases or special sales. For more information, please contact:

U.S. Corporate and Government Sales
1-800-382-3419
corpsales@pearsontechgroup.com

For sales outside of the United States, please contact:

International Sales
international@pearsoned.com

ASSOCIATE PUBLISHER	PROJECT EDITOR	TECHNICAL EDITORS	MULTIMEDIA
Mark Taber	Dan Knott	Max Mether	DEVELOPER
		MySQL AB	Dan Scherf
ACQUISITIONS EDITOR	COPY EDITOR		
Shelley Johnston	Kitty Jarrett	PUBLISHING	DESIGNER
		COORDINATOR	Gary Adair
DEVELOPMENT EDITOR	INDEXER	Vanessa Evans	
Damon Jordan	Bill Meyers		PAGE LAYOUT
			Brad Chinn
MANAGING EDITOR	PROOFREADER		
Charlotte Clapp	Elizabeth Scott		

MySQL® Press is the exclusive publisher of technology books and materials that have been authorized by MySQL AB. MySQL Press books are written and reviewed by the world's leading authorities on MySQL technologies, and are edited, produced, and distributed by the Que/Sams Publishing group of Pearson Education, the worldwide leader in integrated education and computer technology publishing. For more information on MySQL Press and MySQL Press books, please go to www.mysqlpress.com.

MYSQL HQ
MySQL AB
Bangårdsgatan 8
S-753 20 Uppsala
Sweden

UNITED STATES
MySQL Inc.
2510 Fairview Avenue East
Seattle, WA 98102
USA

GERMANY, AUSTRIA AND SWITZERLAND
MySQL GmbH
Schlosserstraße 4
D-72622 Nürtingen
Germany

FINLAND
MySQL Finland Oy
Tekniikantie 21
FIN-02150 Espoo
Finland

FRANCE
MySQL AB (France)
123, rue du Faubourg St. Antoine
75011, Paris
France

MySQL® AB develops, markets, and supports a family of high-performance, affordable database servers and tools. MySQL AB is the sole owner of the MySQL server source code, the MySQL trademark, and the mysql.com domain. For information on MySQL AB and MySQL AB products, please go to www.mysql.com or the following areas of the MySQL website:

- Training information: **www.mysql.com/training**
- Support services: **www.mysql.com/support**
- Consulting services: **www.mysql.com/consulting**

About the Authors

Alex Davies is a student reading economics at Durham University in the United Kingdom. He has worked as a freelance systems administrator specializing in clustering since 2000, and he is a member of the exclusive MySQL Guilds for "exceptional MySQL Community members."

Alex is a regular participant on the MySQL Cluster mailing lists and forums and has helped hundreds of people with their clusters.

When not in front of a computer, Alex enjoys sports, including cross-country running and adventure training, particularly walking, climbing, and skiing.

Harrison Fisk is employed as a consultant and trainer by MySQL AB. He teaches many MySQL Cluster and general MySQL courses throughout the United States and Canada. In addition, he occasionally gives talks at conferences and meetings dealing with MySQL Cluster and MySQL in general. You can regularly find him interacting with the MySQL community through IRC, forums, and mailing lists.

Harrison lives with his fiancée and soulmate, Erin, and their two cats, Neko and Forrest. When not working, he enjoys video games, going to the movies, and playing role-playing games.

Acknowledgments

More people have contributed to this book than I can possibly mention here. MySQL Community members who helped me as they continue to help others get started and to explain both technical and silly questions with infinite patience. Mikael Ronström and Stewart Smith have been exceptionally generous with their time.

I also reserve special thanks to Arjen Lentz (community relations manager for MySQL AB), who published my first guide on http://dev.mysql.com (which led to this book) and who has continued to provide me with opportunities to get involved with the MySQL community.

I also owe a huge debt of gratitude to my co-author, who has continually corrected my errors and helped me with all sorts of details during the process of writing this book.

Finally I thank everyone who allowed me the time to complete this project, including everyone at Oundle (particularly Bruce McDowell for encouraging me to work hard at what I was good at) and of course my parents, who lost sight of me for days on end while I was writing this book!

—Alex Davies

Many people have contributed to helping with this book and helping get me where I am today.

First are the MySQL Cluster people themselves, who have spent a lot of time helping me and also in creating this great technology. Mikael, Pekka, Jonas, Martin, Stewart, Jon, and others have all done a great job getting MySQL Cluster where it is now.

Next are the current and former MySQL AB folks, who I thank for creating the original basis for the software and giving me a job where I can learn about things such as MySQL Cluster. Particular thanks to Jeremy, Ulf, Marc, Max, Monty, Kaj, Dean, and Arjen for everything you've done for me over the years.

Additionally, I would like to thank my co-author and editor, who have put up with me and my procrastination for the duration of the book process. I find their patience to be very generous and understanding, and I have enjoyed working with them.

Finally, thanks to the non-MySQL people who have helped me out so much. My family and friends have all been helpful in keeping me going while writing the book. Erin, my lovely fiancee, has been wonderful and understanding about the time required. Wyatt, one of my best friends, thanks for originally convincing me that writing a book was a good thing.

—Harrison Fisk

Contents At a Glance

Table of Contents

We Want to Hear from You!

As the reader of this book, *you* are our most important critic and commentator. We value your opinion and want to know what we're doing right, what we could do better, what areas you'd like to see us publish in, and any other words of wisdom you're willing to pass our way.

You can email or write me directly to let me know what you did or didn't like about this book—as well as what we can do to make our books stronger.

Please note that I cannot help you with technical problems related to the topic of this book, and that due to the high volume of mail I receive, I might not be able to reply to every message.

When you write, please be sure to include this book's title and author as well as your name and phone number or email address. I will carefully review your comments and share them with the author and editors who worked on the book.

Email: mysqlpress@pearsoned.com

Mail: Mark Taber
            Associate Publisher
            Pearson Education/MySQL Press
            800 East 96th Street
            Indianapolis, IN 46240 USA

Introduction

MySQL Cluster is an enterprise-grade, scalable, and highly available clustering product from MySQL AB, released under the MySQL dual license. MySQL Cluster is a share-nothing cluster with no single point of failure, and it is capable of running on inexpensive commodity hardware. MySQL Cluster allows the construction of cheap, scalable, and exceptionally reliable database clusters, without additional expensive specialized hardware or software. This makes MySQL Cluster a unique product.

It is possible to achieve telco-grade "five nines" uptime (99.999%) by using MySQL Cluster if you plan, deploy, and manage your cluster correctly. Managing a cluster in MySQL Cluster is a big step up from managing a classic MySQL server, and this book explains how MySQL Cluster works, taking you through the process of installing a cluster and explaining how best to manage it.

This book is *not* a "quick-start" guide. Simple guides on how to set up a very basic cluster can be found at MySQL's excellent developer site, http://dev.mysql.com. This book explains everything you need to know as a new cluster administrator. It assumes that you have basic knowledge of how MySQL and Linux in general work. Although some other platforms are supported (note that Windows is not included on this list), we do not explicitly cover these; the process for these platforms is very similar. We strongly recommend that you deploy your cluster using a recent version of Linux.

This book requires a little more patience and time than most introductory books simply due to the complexity of the underlying subject matter. You will experience a massive learning curve as you learn more and more about MySQL Cluster, and this book makes that curve significantly steeper. Experience shows that users who actually understand what they are doing rather than just following sample commands make far better administrators, and this is especially true with a complex piece of software such as MySQL Cluster.

This introduction first introduces you to MySQL Cluster and gives you a rough idea of its capabilities and limitations. It then introduces what this book covers.

Introduction to Database Clustering

In a classic MySQL database, rows of data are arranged in columns to form tables. These tables are stored in files on the disk of the database server, and queries are made to them. If the server crashes, the database goes down. If the load from all the queries gets too large, the only solution is to make the server more powerful.

Clustering spreads processing over multiple servers, resulting in a single redundant (that is, not reliant on any one single machine) and scalable (that is, you can add more machines) solution. A cluster in MySQL Cluster consists of a set of computers that run MySQL servers to receive and respond to queries, storage nodes to store the data held in the cluster and to process the queries, and one or more management nodes to act as a central point to manage the entire cluster. There are many reasons for clustering a database and several different methods of clustering.

The distinction between scaling up and scaling out is worth explaining. *Scaling up* is the traditional method that is used when the current hardware hits its limit: Administrators simply upgrade the hardware within the current server or replace it with a more powerful unit. *Scaling out* means that you *add* more servers while keeping your old hardware still in place. Scaling out is generally considered superior in terms of cost and reliability. However, it is much more difficult to set up, and software costs can be higher. Clusters in MySQL Cluster scale out (that is, they take what normally is powered by one server and spread it out over multiple servers). They are far more complicated to run than a standard MySQL server, but once correctly deployed, they provide the most cost-effective and reliable database cluster available. It is always worth remembering that support contracts are available from MySQL AB for deployments that require the additional guarantee of 24x7 support.

Why Cluster a Database?

There are two main reasons to cluster a database. The first is to allow the complete failure of individual servers within the cluster, without any downtime to the users of the database (that is, redundancy). The second is to allow more hardware to be added to the cluster—transparently to the users of the database—to increase performance (that is, scalability). This allows the database to be run on a large number of inexpensive machines, and it allows inexpensive machines to be added to the cluster as and when they are required.

There are other advantages of a cluster in MySQL Cluster compared to alternatives such as separate database servers with partitioned data, advanced replication setups, and other database clusters, including easier management (for example, all nodes in a cluster can be controlled from one single machine), lower costs, and greater reliability. It is also much easier to back up a large cluster than lots of separate database servers each serving up a partition of the data.

Types of Clustering

There are two main methods of clustering a database: shared-nothing and shared-disk clustering. There are also shared-memory clusters, which you can use if you use Dolphin SCI Interconnects with MySQL Cluster, which is covered later on in this book.

Shared-Disk Clustering

Shared-disk clustering means that multiple database servers actually read from the same disk (for example, a RAID array within a storage area network [SAN]). The challenge with this model is ensuring that no node undoes the work of another, which typically requires global memory and lock management. The lock manager must communicate with all the nodes on every transaction. As you might expect, the lock manager can quickly become the limiting factor in shared-disk scalability! Shared-disk clustering is used by Oracle Parallel Server and can be used by IBM's DB2.

Shared-Nothing Clustering

Shared-nothing clustering was developed in response to the limitations of shared-disk clustering. Each server owns its own disk resources (that is, they share nothing at any point in time). To maintain high availability, the cluster software monitors the health of each server in the cluster. In the event of a failure, the other servers in the cluster take over the job from the crashed server, transparently to the user of the database. This provides the same high level of availability as shared-disk clustering, and it provides potentially higher scalability because it does not have the inherent bottleneck of a lock manager.

Shared-nothing clustering is generally considered superior to shared-disk clustering; however, it clearly requires far more complex software. MySQL clustering is shared-nothing clustering.

Replication Versus Clustering

MySQL has a feature known as *replication* that many confuse with clustering. *Replication* is server-implemented technology that protects against database failure by mirroring changes on a secondary server. It also provides a second access point for data that can protect against link failures and can share the load in high-traffic situations. However, the slave(s) must be read-only, so this still leaves the problem of a single point of failure as well as requiring a very powerful master machine because this machine must deal with all the write queries as well as the queries from the multiple slave machines in order to keep them all in sync. It is therefore not particularly scalable (the number of write operations that can be conducted is determined by the hardware of the master node) or highly available (if the master node dies, in most situations, at the very least, all write operations will fail).

There are many problems with trying to make replication highly available—mainly problems with primary keys. Replication is also asynchronous, which means that data is transmitted intermittently rather than in a steady stream. While there are "botches" to get replication to act as a cluster, MySQL Cluster is the only true solution for situations that require high availability and scalability.

Hardware Considerations with MySQL Cluster

MySQL Cluster is an *in-memory system*, which means it operates out of system RAM. For reasons that are explained later, the following is a rough guideline of the RAM required for a simple cluster:

Maximum Potential Size of One Row × 1.1 × 2 × number of rows

MySQL Cluster in MySQL 4.1 and 5.0 is not efficient at storing VARCHAR, TEXT, or BLOB fields (it treats them all as full-length fields), although this problem is due to be fixed in version 5.1. You also need to include RAM for indexes, and you will see how to calculate the storage requirements in more detail later on. Suffice it to say for now that MySQL Cluster is a RAM-heavy application, and if you have a large database, you need a very large amount of RAM or a very large number of nodes: you can, of course, spread the large total amount of RAM required over many different physical servers.

Despite the fact that a cluster is RAM intensive, there is still a lot of disk activity because each member of the cluster keeps a fairly recent copy of its data on a local disk so that if all nodes crash (complete cluster shutdown) the cluster can recover fairly quickly. Therefore, for really optimum performance, RAID 1 and/or SCSI drives are recommended.

MySQL AB recommends the following hardware for servers acting as storage nodes in the cluster:

- **Operating system**—Linux (Red Hat, SUSE), Solaris, AIX, HP-UX, Mac OS X
- **CPU**—2x Intel Xeon, Intel Itanium, AMD Opteron, Sun SPARC, IBM PowerPC
- **Memory**—16GB RAM
- **Hard disk drive**—4x 36GB SCSI (RAID 1 controller)
- **Network**—1–8 nodes for Gigabit Ethernet; 8 or more nodes for Dedicated Cluster Interconnect

Networking Considerations with MySQL Cluster

A significant amount of traffic is transferred between servers within a cluster, so any latency between nodes is a very bad thing for performance. For this reason, MySQL Cluster is not suited to geographically diverse clusters. Rather, MySQL Cluster is intended to be used in a high-bandwidth environment, with computers typically connected via TCP/IP. Its performance depends directly on the connection speed between the cluster's computers. The minimum connectivity requirements for clusters include a typical 100Mbps Ethernet network or the equivalent. Gigabit Ethernet should be used if available.

Ideally, all the nodes in the cluster should be connected to a switch that is devoted just to the cluster traffic. (There are other reasons to take this approach, apart from performance, as you will see later on.) For enhanced reliability, you can use dual switches and dual cards to remove the network as a single point of failure; many device drivers support failover for such communication links.

MySQL Cluster supports high-speed Scalable Coherent Interface (SCI) interconnects. For clusters with eight or more servers, SCI interconnects are recommended. We will talk about these in more detail later on.

Why Use a MySQL Cluster?

Using MySQL Cluster has many advantages over running standalone MySQL servers. The following sections discuss three advantages—high availability, scalability, and performance—and briefly touch on some other advantages.

High Availability

Many administrators of MySQL servers are looking for enormous uptimes. The maximum that it is sensible to aim for in most cases is five nines (that is, 5.3 minutes downtime a year). This simply is not possible without redundancy, and, as we have seen, the only practical method of redundancy for MySQL is to use a cluster. This is because any one machine—regardless of how many "redundant" power supplies, hard drives, and CPUs it has—will fail occasionally; there is no such thing as an invincible server! The only way to eliminate this problem is to use share-nothing clustering. This way, it takes more than one failure to bring down the cluster, and the probability of an unusual event (such as a power supply or disk drive failure) occurring on two machines at exactly the same time is small enough to ignore. (Of course, you can design a cluster that can survive three or more concurrent failures, but you take a performance hit for this sort of setup.)

High availability means being able to suffer power supply or hard drive failures without any downtime to your users. It means being able to take servers down for upgrades while your database remains up. It means upgrading the database software without any downtime. All this is possible only with a clustering product such as MySQL Cluster. Note that some of these features—such as upgrades without downtime—are currently not supported within MySQL Cluster but are high up on the to-do list.

Scalability

Scalability is important because it allows you to increase your hardware costs as your database is used more. Put simply, it means that when you launch your database, you can start off with not very much hardware, and the hardware you use can be inexpensive. If you find that demand for your data is enormous, you can add a lot more hardware very quickly. At the moment, the addition of extra nodes requires a total cluster restart, but this should be fixed in MySQL 5.1.

One of MySQL Cluster's great features is near-linear scalability, so a two-server cluster will handle almost exactly half the load of a four-server cluster.

Performance

Sometimes MySQL Cluster does not result in higher performance, but in many cases it does. Queries that can be split up and run in parallel run much faster on a cluster in MySQL Cluster than on a single MySQL box because MySQL Cluster runs the bits in parallel on different storage nodes. If you have queries that can not be split up and run in parallel, MySQL Cluster has to run them on one storage node, and clearly this is slower due to the additional networking overheads of a cluster.

Other Advanced Features

One problem with MySQL is the difficulty of making backups without locking files for fairly significant periods of time. To combat this problem, MySQL Cluster features hot online backups, which allows administrators to make backups while a cluster is running, without locking tables. This is one of the many features that make MySQL Cluster a product that can compete with vastly more expensive databases, such as Oracle and IBM DB/2.

MySQL Cluster features extremely fast (subsecond) failover in the event of a node failure. It features good management tools that, with the help of this book, allow administrators to manage a cluster with ease.

MySQL Cluster also supports simple parallel query processing. The cluster engine used for MySQL Cluster also provides full support for transactions; indeed, any nontransaction queries automatically have transactions wrapped around them.

Cluster Terminology

There are several significant terms that any administrator must come to grips with early on when using MySQL Cluster. The three different types of nodes are storage, SQL, and management nodes. The following sections discuss their different roles within a cluster. We will also talk about the differences between the storage engine within a cluster compared to two other common engines: MyISAM and InnoDB.

How a MySQL Cluster Works

MySQL Cluster consists of standard MySQL daemons and special daemons that control the storage and execution of queries in the background. These two different parts can run on the same servers or different servers. However, there must be at least one standard MySQL server and two background nodes running, spread out over at least two servers. A third server is always required as an arbitrator (as you shall see shortly), so the minimum number of servers on which you can set up a highly available cluster in MySQL Cluster is three.

> **Note**
> Many people find the requirement for three servers impossible to believe and try to set up two-server clusters. However, you must have at least three physical servers to set up a highly available cluster in MySQL Cluster. It is not possible to do with two servers. We explain the reason for this later on in the book.

In simple terms, a query comes into a standard MySQL daemon and is then sent to a background daemon (that is, a "storage node"). This daemons decides whether to answer the query alone or with other storage nodes (for greater speed) if the query is read-only, or if the query is a write or update query, it initiates the write as part of a transaction on all storage nodes and undergoes a two-phase commit process to ensure that all the other storage nodes have received and acted on the write.

Different Parts of a Cluster in MySQL Cluster

MySQL Cluster has three separate types of nodes (that is, services that form part of a cluster): storage nodes, SQL nodes, and management nodes. Nodes run on servers, and you can run multiple nodes on one physical server, subject to the limitations discussed later in this introduction.

Storage Nodes

Storage nodes store the fragments of data that make up the tables held in a cluster and do the early work in processing queries. Storage nodes require a large amount of RAM and relatively high-performance machines. The bulk of the processing is done on the storage nodes, and these are the nodes that an administrator spends most of his or her time tweaking. They are completely controlled from the management node via the configuration file and management client.

SQL Nodes

SQL nodes, which run on standard MySQL servers, are the nodes that applications can connect to. In small, simple clusters, these nodes are often run on the same physical servers as the storage nodes. Essentially, SQL nodes provide the "face" to the cluster and operate exactly as standard MySQL servers. They then connect to the storage nodes behind, which do the early processing on the queries and return the results for final processing at the SQL nodes. The amount of processing done on the SQL and storage nodes changes from query to query.

Management Nodes

Management nodes have two important roles: First, in most setups, they act as arbitrators if there are any networking problems between cluster nodes to decide which part of the cluster should remain alive. Second, they also are required when starting any other node in a cluster (they hold the configuration that each cluster node requires each time it starts), and they manage online backups. You can stop and restart storage and management nodes by issuing a signal from the management console, and you use the management server to get information about the current status of the cluster. You also use the management client as a central log of what is going on with the cluster. A cluster typically has one management node, although it is possible to have multiple management nodes.

The MySQL Cluster Storage Engine

You may be familiar with the classic storage engines of MySQL: MyISAM and InnoDB. MyISAM is very good at read-heavy environments, and InnoDB has transaction and other advanced feature support. MySQL Cluster uses neither of these; instead, it uses a transaction engine called Network Database (NDB). NDB was designed specifically for MySQL Cluster and for distribution over multiple storage nodes. It is in-memory (RAM) and so is very fast because it does not have the traditional bottlenecks of disk I/O.

MyISAM Versus NDB

Table IN.1 shows the key differences between MyISAM, the default storage engine in MySQL, and NDB, the only available storage engine with MySQL Cluster.

TABLE IN.1   **MyISAM Versus NDB**

Feature	MyISAM	NDB
Supports multistatement transactions and rollbacks	No	Yes
Supports full-text indexes	Yes	No
Can use hash lookups	No	Yes
Supports Unicode from version	4.1	5.0
Can compress read-only storage	Yes	No
Supports foreign keys	Yes	No
Uses a lot of RAM and has a lot of network traffic	No	Yes

InnoDB Versus NDB

Table IN.2 shows the key differences between InnoDB, the storage engine used by those requiring transactions within MySQL, and NDB, the only available storage engine with MySQL Cluster. InnoDB is in many ways more similar to NDB than MyISAM.

TABLE IN.2   InnoDB Versus NDB

Feature	InnoDB	NDB
Supports foreign key constraints	Yes	No
Supports Unicode from version	4.1.2	5.0
Uses a lot of RAM and has a lot of network traffic	No	Yes

Limitations of NDB

NDB has many limitations that are very easy to forget. Some databases cannot convert to NDB without significant modification, and often while importing a large existing database, you meet one of these limitations. Typically, as long as you can work out what limitation you have hit, there are ways around whatever problem you have met, but you should be aware that this is not always the case. The following are some of the possibilities:

- Database names, table names, and attribute names cannot be as long in NDB tables as with other table handlers. In NDB, attribute names are truncated to 31 characters, and if they are not unique after truncation, errors occur. Database names and table names can total a maximum of 122 characters

- NDB does not support prefix indexes; only entire fields can be indexed.

- A big limitation is that in MySQL 4.1 and 5.0, all cluster table rows are of fixed length. This means, for example, that if a table has one or more VARCHAR fields containing only relatively small values, more memory and disk space will be required when using the NDB storage engine than would be for the same table and data using the MyISAM engine. This issue is on the "to-fix" list for MySQL Cluster 5.1.

- In NDB, the maximum number of metadata objects is limited to 20,000, including database tables, system tables, indexes, and BLOBs (binary large objects). This is a hard-coded limit that you cannot override with a configuration option.

- The maximum permitted size of any one row in NDB is 8KB, not including data stored in BLOB columns (which are actually stored in a separate table internally).

- The maximum number of attributes per key in NDB is 32.

- Autodiscovery of databases is not supported in NDB for multiple MySQL servers accessing the same cluster in MySQL Cluster. (You have to add each database manually on each SQL node.)

- MySQL replication does not work correctly in NDB if updates are done on multiple MySQL servers; replication between clusters is on the feature list for MySQL 5.1.

- ALTER TABLE is not fully locking in NDB when you're running multiple MySQL servers.

- All storage and management nodes within a cluster in NDB must have the same architecture. This restriction does not apply to machines simply running SQL nodes or any other clients that may be accessing the cluster.

- It is not possible to make online schema changes in NDB, such as those accomplished using ALTER TABLE or CREATE INDEX. (However, you can import or create a table that uses a different storage engine and then convert it to NDB by using ALTER TABLE *tbl_name* ENGINE=NDBCLUSTER;.) ALTER TABLE works on occasions, but all it does is create a new table with the new structure and then import the data. This generally causes an error as NDB hits a limit somewhere. It is strongly recommended that you not use ALTER TABLE to make online schema changes.

- Adding or removing nodes online is not possible in NDB. (The cluster must be restarted in such cases.)

- The maximum number of storage nodes within an NDB cluster is 48.

- The total maximum number of nodes in a cluster in MySQL Cluster is 63. This number includes all MySQL servers (that is, SQL nodes), storage nodes, and management servers.

Data Partitioning

Data partitioning is an important concept in MySQL Cluster because it explains how a cluster splits up the data that is fed into it among the various storage nodes to achieve high performance and redundancy. Full partitioning, as described here, is available only in MySQL Cluster 5.1. MySQL Cluster 5.0 data is partitioned between storage node groups in a fairly random way.

A partitioned table is an abstract table that implements a table by making use of one stored table for each partition in the table (that is, it splits up one large table into lots of smaller tables). A partition function is a nonconstant and nonrandom function (typically a hash function) of one or more fields in the table; in MySQL Cluster, it is always the primary key. It cannot contain a query but can contain any scalar expression. Currently, the function needs to return an integer result. In addition, the partition function should be relatively simple because it will be evaluated very often in queries.

It is worth bearing in mind that MySQL Cluster automatically adds a primary key to any table that does not have one because it requires one for partitioning.

Benefits of Partitioning

Partitioning is essential in all clusters except clusters where the number of replicas is equal to the number of storage nodes because somehow the cluster must split the data equally across all the node groups. For example, if there are four nodes and two copies of every piece of data (that is, replicas), each node holds half the total data, and a partitioning function is required to decide where each piece of data can be found.

Certain queries can therefore be much more efficient. For example, consider the following query:

```
SELECT field1 FROM table1 WHERE id = 46;
```

If id were the primary key, the cluster would know immediately after running the partitioning function on the integer 46 which node group to send this query to for fast processing because the other node groups could never contain any records that would satisfy the WHERE clause.

Partitioning in general lays a foundation for parallel query support (that is queries executed on multiple nodes at the same time). For example, it is very simple to parallelize the query:

```
SELECT SUM(some_data) WHERE some_data > 100;
```

This query can be executed in parallel on each node, and the total sum is the sum of the query executed against each individual partition, resulting in the same answer being returned to the application much more quickly.

Synchronous Replication

Synchronous replication means that queries do not complete until the changes have been applied to all the servers involved. This has the benefit of guaranteeing that all servers have consistent copies of the data, but it can be a real performance problem, even though it eliminates the time-consuming operation of re-creating and replaying log files required by shared-disk architectures to fail over successfully.

This effectively means that when a MySQL Cluster node receives a write query (that is, a query that requires it to change its fragment of data), it issues the query on both itself and the other node(s) that holds this fragment of data. A transaction coordinator, chosen randomly from all the storage nodes, waits for the other node(s) to confirm acceptance of the transaction before issuing a commit and also confirming to the SQL node that issued the query that the transaction completed successfully.

Node Groups

MySQL Cluster automatically splits nodes into node groups. The size of each node group is determined by the number of copies of each fragment of data that the cluster holds (which is configurable but is typically set to 2). So, if you have two copies of data, each node group has two nodes in it. As long as one node within each node group survives, the cluster will survive. Each node within a node group has identical data; consequently, as long as one node in each node group is alive, the cluster remains up because it has a complete set of data.

A Practical Example of Partitioning and Node Groups

Figure IN.1 shows two servers running four storage nodes on two physical machines. Physical Machine 1 is running Storage Node 1 and Storage Node 3, and Physical Machine 2 is running Storage Node 2 and Storage Node 4.

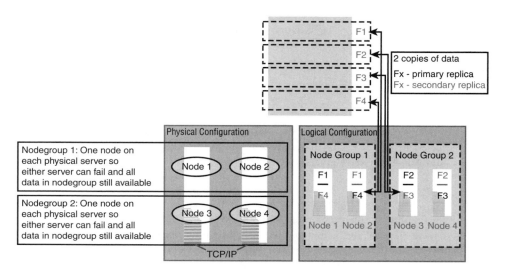

FIGURE IN.1   Two physical servers, with two storage nodes on each server, for a total of four storage nodes. With two replicas of each piece of data, we have two node groups. Either server can fail, and the database will remain up.

The four storage nodes are split into two node groups, with Storage Nodes 1 and 2 making up Node Group 1 and Storage Nodes 3 and 4 making up Node Group 2.

Already, you can see that each physical server has one node from each node group on it—so a failure of either server still leaves one complete node group working on the other server.

Four items of data, F1 through to F4 (Fragments 1 through 4) are stored on this simple cluster. Each fragment of data has two copies—within the same node group. So Data Fragment 1 has a copy on Storage Node 1 (which is on Physical Server 1) and also a copy on Storage Node 2 (which is on Physical Server 2). You should notice how this is redundant: Either physical server could die, and the piece of data would remain available. You can put your finger over any one node in Figure IN.1 to convince yourself.

Network Partitioning and Arbitration

There is a fundamental problem with all clusters: If they get split in half, one half must shut down (or at least enter read-only mode) to prevent the two remaining halves from continuing to work and getting separate copies of the database, which would be difficult or impossible to merge at a later date. This problem is known as the "split-brain" problem.

MySQL solves this problem in a very simple way. First, as mentioned earlier, you must always have at least three physical servers in a cluster in MySQL Cluster for your cluster to be highly available; it is not possible to set up a highly available cluster with two (because otherwise, the cluster would be subject to the split-brain problem). A simplified explanation of how MySQL solves this problem goes like this: When nodes go down in a cluster, you have either majority rules (that is, if more than half of the nodes can see each other, they are the cluster) or, in a case in which you have an even number of nodes (such as 4) and only two nodes can see each other, it's whoever has the arbitrator. Note that the arbitrator is typically the management node. Note that we refer to a highly available cluster here: It is technically possible to set up a cluster with two or even one node, but doing so is pointless because it means you miss out on the main benefit of MySQL Cluster—high availability—and yet suffer all the overheads of a cluster.

A more complicated explanation of split-brain scenarios is required when you consider that the cluster is split into node groups. When all nodes in at least one node group are alive, it is not possible to get network partitioning. In this case, no other cluster half can form a functional cluster (because it would be missing the set of data that is in the node group that can still see the other). The problem comes when no node group has all its nodes alive because in that case, network partitioning is technically possible. In this situation, an arbitrator is contacted. The nodes in the cluster select the arbitrator before the node failure (during the startup process) so that all nodes will contact the same arbitrator. Normally the arbitrator would be the management server, but it can also be configured to be any of the MySQL servers in the cluster. The arbitrator will accept only the first cluster half to contact to survive. The second half will be told to die. Nodes that cannot connect to the arbitrator after a certain period of time automatically die, thus preventing a split-brain scenario.

The problem with network partitioning is that a highly available cluster can be formed only if at least three computers are involved in the cluster. One of those computers is needed only to handle the arbitrator function, so there is no need for high performance of any kind in this computer. This is because if you have only two nodes and they are unable to contact each other, which half should die? How does one node know if the other node has crashed or suffered a hardware failure or if there is a networking problem between them? It can't, so in such a cluster, both nodes die.

A Brief History of MySQL Cluster

The initial design, prototypes, and research for MySQL Cluster were completed between 1991 and 1996 by a company called Alzato that was started by Ericcson. Most of the code today originates from 1996. The first demo of MySQL Cluster came in 1997, and since then, the feature set and reliability have increased massively. Version 1.0 came out in April 2001, with Perl DBI support. In version 1.4, in 2002, work on node recovery was completed. 2003 brought ODBC, online backup, unique indexes, and more. The most recent features include online upgrades and ordered indexes.

MySQL Cluster is now included with the MySQL-Max package and is also available as a separate package to download from www.mysql.com.

What's New in MySQL Cluster 5.0

All the following features are included in MySQL Cluster version 5.0:

- **Push-down conditions**—A query such as the following:

```
SELECT * FROM t1 WHERE non_indexed_attribute = 1;
```

  uses a full table scan, which under older versions of MySQL Cluster would result in the entire non_indexed_attribute field in the t1 table being sent over the network to the SQL node and then each row being compared with 1. In Cluster 5.0 and later, the condition will be evaluated in the cluster's data nodes. Thus it is not necessary to send the records across the network for evaluation, which clearly increases performance significantly. This feature is disabled by default and can be enabled with the command SET engine-condition-pushdown=On.

- **Decreased IndexMemory usage (compared to earlier versions)**—In MySQL 5.0, each record consumes approximately 25 bytes of index memory, and every unique index uses 25 bytes per record of index memory because there is no storage of the primary key in the index memory. You should be aware that unique indexes also consume DataMemory, as explained in more detail later on.

- **New caches and optimizations**—The query cache has now been enabled, and many new optimizations have been introduced since version 4.1.

- **An increase in some hard limits**—Some hard limits have been increased. For example, there has been a significant increase in the limit on number of metadata objects from 1,600 to more than 20,000.

What's New in MySQL Cluster 5.1

All the following features are planned for release in MySQL Cluster 5.1:

- **Parallel processing for greater performance**—The amount of parallel processing that takes place on each node will be increased, and users will have the ability to define their own partitions and subpartitions.

- **Correct handling of variable-width fields**—In version 5, a column defined as VAR-CHAR(255) uses 260 bytes of storage, independent of what is stored in any particular record. In MySQL 5.1 Cluster tables, only the portion of the field actually taken up by the record will be stored. In many cases, this will make possible a reduction in space requirements for such columns by a factor of five.

- **Replication between clusters**—MySQL also hopes to integrate replication into clustering so you will be able to have replication slaves within a cluster.

- **Disk-based tables**—Disk-based tables are planned and are in early testing at the time of this writing; they will remove the current limitation that you must have at least 2.1 times your database size in RAM to run MySQL Cluster. However, you will still need indexes in RAM, and disk-based tables will likely reduce performance significantly.

Designing a Cluster

The following sections cover the essential things you should consider when designing a cluster. It is very important to design a cluster correctly before you start trying to use it; trying to run a cluster with two machines in different offices connected via the Internet will not work, nor will trying to import 2GB of data if you have only 1GB of RAM.

Networking

You need to connect all your nodes with at least a 100Mbps network connection. You are strongly advised to use a dedicated network for cluster traffic (that is, have two network cards in each node, eth0 and eth1, and use one of them for MySQL Cluster and the other for everything else). If you plan on having a cluster with a significant amount of traffic, you should use Gigabit Ethernet.

You should not try to set up cluster nodes all over a WAN such as the Internet. It won't work—nodes constantly communicate with each other using small pieces of information called heartbeats. The main role of a heartbeat is to ask the question "are you alive?" The receiving node simply sends another one back. As long as each node gets a heartbeat from each other node within the timeout value specified in the main configuration file, the cluster remains up. In a WAN, a large number of these heartbeats go missing or get delayed during transit, and the cluster ends up breaking very quickly.

Determining the Number of Replicas

A major decision is how redundant and fast you want your cluster; the more redundant and fast it is, the more RAM and hardware you need. The parameter `NumberOfReplicas` determines how many times MySQL Cluster stores each piece of data. To have a highly available cluster, you need at least two replicas, and this is the conventional value.

Just having more replicas does not automatically mean that you achieve higher performance. In fact, the law of diminishing returns kicks in fairly quickly, particularly if you have a write-heavy system (because each write must be committed `NumberOfReplicas` times before the transaction can be closed to the client, and although this happens in parallel, the more transactions that are going on, the longer it is likely to take), and it is unusual to have a value greater than 4 for `NumberOfReplicas`.

Determining the Amount of RAM

Having decided how many replicas you want, you need to decide how many nodes you need. The most important factor in this is RAM; you need to find your total RAM requirement and then divide that by the amount of RAM you have in each machine to work out how many nodes you require. As you have already seen, this is a rough estimate of RAM usage for a "typical" cluster:

Data Size × `NumberOfReplicas` × 1.1

It should be noted that your RAM usage can be massively larger in several situations, and if you have lots of indexes, you should consider changing 1.1 to something much larger, such as 1.5.

As a practical example, say you have a row size of 100KB and 100,000 rows. That is just under 1000MB or 1GB of data size. Say you have decided that you want four replicas. The rough estimate of RAM would be $1,000 \times 4 \times 1.1 = 4,400$, or 4.4GB.

If you have machines that can take 2GB of RAM, you want 2.2 machines. You clearly can't have 2.2 machines, so you round this up to 3. However, your total number of nodes should be a multiple of `NumberOfReplicas`; 3 is a suboptimal number of servers, so we would settle on 4 machines.

You might consider four servers slightly excessive, but there are several points to bear in mind:

- Although there may be 2GB of RAM per storage node, some of this is used by the operating system, and a certain amount of free RAM is important if you want a stable system.
- It is always good to have a significant amount of spare RAM within a cluster so you do not run the risk of running out of RAM and crashing if the amount of data increases for some reason.
- It is safest to round up at every stage. You will use more RAM than you anticipate.

It is strongly recommended for performance reasons that you have 2, 4, 8, or 12 nodes for performance reasons and not any number in between these. If you use other numbers, you will find that the partitioning function struggles to evenly partition the data between nodes, so you will not get well-balanced partitions.

Determining the Amount of Disk Space

You want plenty of disk space free on the storage nodes. The disk will be used for backups as well as regular commits of the data, which are used if the cluster suffers a fatal crash.

If you want fast backups or have a write-heavy application, you should certainly consider using SCSI drives or some sort of RAID solution. If you have only two replicas, you might want to ensure that both nodes remain up for the vast majority of the time for performance reasons, so RAID may be important here as well. Although I/O performance does not directly increase the performance of a cluster, it may help reduce the overall system load if other processes are not waiting around for disk access. If you can afford it, this is highly recommended.

Choosing an Operating System

MySQL Cluster has been run on many diverse operating systems, including Solaris and BSD, as well as Linux. If you want an easy life and just want a cluster to work, you should run all nodes on Linux. This will almost certainly get you the best possible performance and stability.

You can select any Linux distribution you like, although the operating system that most new administrators go with is something like Red Hat Enterprise 4, which is perfectly suited to this. CentOS (www.centos.org) provides a "binary compatible" (that is, identical) version of Red Hat Enterprise Linux (RHEL), which is also complexly free, so if you do not need the support offered by Red Hat, you can use CentOS. Other popular Linux distributions are SUSE and Debian. The chances are very high that whatever versions of Linux you choose, it will come with MySQL preinstalled.

The code for running MySQL Cluster on Windows is not yet complete, and you should not attempt to run MySQL Cluster in a production environment on Windows.

> **A Note on Hardware**
> You should ensure that all your storage nodes are as identical as possible. Although it is possible to have different amounts of RAM on each storage node, we do not advise it. If you have completely identical machines (apart from IP address), having the same amount of RAM on each machine will make management much simpler, and it will make rapid disaster recovery fairly easy. If you have differing amounts of RAM, you will only be able to use the smallest amount of RAM in any storage node on all storage nodes, so the extra RAM will probably just be wasted.

What This Book Covers

This book covers a lot of very complex topics. The following sections briefly explain what you can expect to find in each chapter. The book is designed so you can either dip in and out or read it cover to cover, depending on your existing knowledge, time available, and goals.

Chapter 1, "Installation"

Chapter 1 covers installing MySQL Cluster. This includes the basic installation process, either from binaries or from source. Chapter 1 covers the differences in the process between the various different versions, and it shows how to install the cutting-edge nightly builds. Although you'll learn about advanced configuration later, Chapter 1 introduces you to the various configuration files you will later become familiar with, when you use them to get your cluster up and running.

Chapter 1 also covers some common installation problems and the best methods for upgrading a cluster in a live environment. More complex installation scenarios, such as disaster recovery, are covered in later chapters but require a strong understanding of how to install the software.

Finally, Chapter 1 covers importing your current tables into the new cluster, as well as some of the common problems that can occur during this process. This process is more complex than it sounds, and you should not expect it to be as simple as you might have hoped, unless your table structure is exceptionally simple.

Chapter 2, "Configuration"

When you have a basic cluster installed, you need to be able to configure it. Chapter 2 introduces you to the hundreds of configuration options you can set to control all aspects of a cluster. It explains them all in clear English so you know exactly what you can configure and where.

Chapter 2 explains how to calculate the size of a database and how to work out how many storage nodes you require and how much RAM you need in each. It then explains the advanced configuration options you are likely to want to use at some stage. Finally, Chapter 2 explains all the complex options you are unlikely to need—just in case you are inquisitive, like to control everything, or come across a situation where you need to configure these options.

Chapter 2 also gives you some examples of configuration files that you can use as a base for your configuration, which should speed up the process of setting up a cluster.

Chapter 3, "Backup and Recovery"

Chapter 3 covers the topic of backing up and restoring a new cluster, including recovering from various scenarios. Many features have been added to MySQL Cluster that will make backing up and restoring a cluster a very neat and easy process.

MySQL Cluster includes support for hot online backups, and this is one of the major features that most MySQL administrators have been wishing for! Of course, no backup is good unless the disaster recovery process is smooth, and Chapter 3 covers this in detail, describing the different disasters you could potentially have to restore from and the best method to use in each case.

Chapter 4, "Security and Management"

Chapter 4 covers two important topics: advanced usage of the management console to help manage a cluster and securing a cluster. Securing a cluster is vital because MySQL Cluster provides absolutely no security, and you must add your own if you want to use it in a production environment.

Having a good working knowledge of all the commands you can issue to the management console is critical for efficient management of a cluster because it is the only sensible way of communicating with individual nodes.

Security is vital, and Chapter 4 discusses many different tricks and tips that are not actually part of MySQL Cluster. It is no exaggeration to say that there is not a single bit of security in MySQL Cluster, so you have to ensure that your cluster is secure by using other applications, such as firewalls, and additional hardware, such as dedicated networks for cluster traffic.

Chapter 5, "Performance"

After a cluster is installed, configured, backed up, and secured, it is then important to get as much performance out of it as you can. Chapter 5 shows you the many different ways of increasing the performance of a cluster.

There are so many different ways that you can optimize a database that Chapter 5 is vital reading. Because there are so many different uses for a database, some of the suggestions in Chapter 5 might not make sense in your situation, but you should be able to significantly increase the performance of your cluster if you follow a few of the suggestions. Performance is even more critical with a cluster than with a standard MySQL server. Whereas a standard MySQL installation will perform fairly well most of the time with a default installation, this is not the case with a cluster; if you do not make any effort to tweak the performance of a cluster, the chances are very high that you will get exceptionally poor performance or require expensive hardware to get good performance.

As well as showing you how to increase performance of a cluster, Chapter 5 also shows you how to stress-test the cluster with various different tools, and it also describes the different ways of automatically monitoring of a cluster so that you know when any dragons appear before they rear their heads and become apparent to your users. This is of critical importance if you plan to use a cluster in a production environment because there is no nice centralized GUI for MySQL Cluster; you have to write scripts and regularly check things manually to ensure that a cluster is working as you expect.

Chapter 6, "Troubleshooting"

Chapter 6 describes solutions to the most common problems users meet when using MySQL Cluster. You should check here before you post on the mailing lists or give up! Working with MySQL Cluster is frustrating at times, and Chapter 6 covers a few of the problems that many users run into time and time again.

Chances are that during your experimentation with MySQL Cluster, you will run into a problem that you may not understand. The trick is always to look for clues—error numbers in log files, for example—and then look for solutions either in Chapter 6 or on the Internet. Chapter 6 covers the basic troubleshooting steps you should carry out if you have a problem, including where error logs are likely to be held as well as how to ask for help or submit a bug report.

Chapter 7, "Common Setups"

Chapter 7 gives you some advice about some very common setups that many users have. Chances are that the scenario in which you plan to use your cluster is either identical or very similar to one of the setups in this chapter.

You may find it helpful, even if your eventual setup is not in this chapter, to try one of these setups first so you can get to know how it works before plunging in and designing your own setup.

Software Versions

Writing a book on any piece of software is a challenge, but on a brand-new piece of software such as MySQL Cluster, it is especially difficult due to the fantastic speed of change. New features are constantly added, and many current features are slightly changing all the time.

Most of the writing of this book was carried out before MySQL 5.0 left beta testing, but we expect that MySQL 5.0 will remain the stable version for some time to come. If you use version 5.1 when it becomes stable, we anticipate that it will be backward compatible, and where it is not, we try to mention it in this book so you should be able to follow this book with ease if you are using either MySQL Cluster 5.0 or 5.1.

More Sources of Information

Apart from this book, there are several other sources of information that we recommend if you want to explore something in more detail or if you get stuck:

- You can find the official MySQL Cluster documentation at http://dev.mysql.com/doc/ mysql/en/ndbcluster.html.
- You can browse the mailing list archive at http://lists.mysql.com/cluster/.
- The MySQL forum contains a cluster forum that you can find at http://forums. mysql.com/list.php?25.

You will also find that there are a large number of posts about MySQL on the Internet, and with a quick Internet search, you can often quickly find people who have had the same problem you're facing.

Installation

Before you try to install a cluster, it is important that you know how a cluster in MySQL Cluster spreads out over multiple computers. It does so by creating three different types of nodes, which do three different jobs:

- **Storage nodes**—These nodes hold the data in the cluster and do most of the actual work processing queries.
- **Management nodes**—These nodes keep the configuration of the cluster and provide a central point from which to manage the cluster.
- **SQL nodes**—These nodes are typically MySQL daemons that accept, parse, and optimize queries and do some of the processing work before returning the results. Some binaries that you will meet later on (such as `ndb_restore` for restoring backups) are also SQL nodes because they connect to the cluster; however, they have little to do with SQL queries.

You can run SQL nodes on the same physical machine as storage and management nodes— and you can run more than one storage node on each physical machine. However, if you want a highly available, fault-tolerant cluster with no single point of failure, you must have at least three physical machines and a management node that does not share a physical machine with a storage node.

The following section discusses a standard installation with the cluster communicating over TCP/IP. Later chapters cover some slightly more complex setups involving high-speed interconnects.

Before You Begin with MySQL Cluster

Before you install or use MySQL Cluster, you should read the section "Limitations of NDB" in this book's introduction, which explains several limitations of current versions of MySQL Cluster that you cannot avoid. Here is a short list of things you should check before you attempt to install or use MySQL Cluster for a project (if you are just setting up a test database as a proof of concept, you can skip this part):

- **Ethernet**—Make sure you have operable networking between all the nodes in the cluster and make sure that any firewalls you have are disabled while you are installing and testing. (Chapter 4, "Security and Management," covers the rules you need to add to your firewall.)

- **RAM**—Make sure you have plenty of RAM free on the servers you plan to use as storage nodes. The Linux command `free -m` tells you how much RAM you have free. As in the following example, you can add the `free` and `cached` columns to get a (very) rough (and high) estimate of available RAM, in megabytes:

```
[root@host] free -m
             total      used      free    shared    buffers     cached
Mem:          3956      3471       484         0        199       2638
-/+ buffers/cache:       633      3322
Swap:         2047        22      2024
```

This server has 2638MB + 484MB free, which is just over 3GB.

- **Table structure**—If you are attempting to move an existing database from MyISAM or InnoDB (or any other storage engine), you might find that it requires some changes. The main limitations are that enormous tables (that is, enormous in the width of each row) will not work; there is a hard-coded limit of 8KB per row (not including data stores in BLOB fields; as you will see later on, these are stored differently). Tables can have as many rows as your RAM will allow. You should also remember that variable-width columns become fixed-width columns with an additional overhead, which means that a `VARCHAR(200)` field uses more than 200 bytes per row—even if it has only 2 bytes of information in it. Depending on the character set, it may take up significantly more space; using utf8, for example, this field will take up at least 600 bytes per row. This explains why most tables end up much larger when they are converted to NDB (Network Database, the storage engine that MySQL Cluster uses).

Obtaining and Installing MySQL Cluster

Before you install MySQL Cluster, you should clearly understand the different processes that you have to undertake to set up the three different type of nodes:

- To set up a SQL node, all you need to do is install the MySQL-Max package and add a few lines to `my.cnf`.

- To set up management and storage nodes, you need to install the MySQL Cluster binaries, the names of which all start with `ndb`.

MySQL-Max is needed on all nodes. As described shortly, you should install MySQL-Max on all the nodes that you plan to take part in the cluster before you do anything else.

Designing a Cluster

It is important that you give some thought to the number of physical servers your cluster will require. Shortly, you will see the sample cluster that we use through this book. It is as simple as you can get if you want a highly available setup, and it requires three physical machines.

You will learn later in this chapter how to calculate the RAM usage for your cluster, but this section explains the important decisions you need to make regarding the layout of your new cluster.

First, you have to decide how many copies of each piece of data you would like the cluster to hold. This determines the number of nodes that will be in each node group. (A *node group* is a group of storage nodes that hold the same data.)

Second, you need to decide how many storage nodes should be part of your cluster. This depends on two things:

- **Performance**—The number of storage nodes, all other things remaining equal, is (very nearly) proportional to performance. However, you should bear in mind that the total number of nodes should be the product of the number of copies of each piece of data you just decided on and a power of 2. For example, if you decide to have two copies of each piece of data—as many clusters do—you should have 2, 4, 8, and so on storage nodes.

- **Memory usage**—If you have a database that takes up 45GB in the cluster format (NDB), you are unlikely to want to use two nodes with 45GB RAM plus operating system overhead! You are more likely to use 8 servers with 12GB of RAM per server (assuming that the cluster is set to hold two copies of each piece of data).

  The number of replicas determines the *total* memory usage required; however, you can spread this out over any number of nodes (and therefore servers) from 1 to 62 to keep the amount of memory required per server to an acceptable level. Note that 64 nodes is the maximum total of all nodes—including SQL, management, and storage nodes—so the realistic maximum number of storage nodes is 62 to allow for 1 management and 1 SQL node.

  At this stage, you can estimate your total memory usage based on your current database size (which you can easily determine) if you use the following formula:

  Total size of database in NDB format × Number of replicas × 1.1

  You then divide this figure by the number of nodes to estimate the memory requirement per node. For initial rough calculations, you can treat the size of the database in NDB as being equal to the current size in whatever storage engine the database is held, subject to the caveat that if you use variable-width columns, you should covert your variable-width columns to fixed-width and calculate the new size and then plug the new size in to the preceding formula to get a more accurate estimate. Of course, you can just make a guestimate or use the `ndb_size.pl` script that is discussed shortly.

Later in this chapter, you will learn how to calculate your memory usage far more accurately. The purpose of mentioning this basic formula here is to give you some idea of how much RAM you are likely to need. Bear in mind that this estimate could be off by a long way in some circumstances; many new users are surprised by the amount of RAM that a MySQL cluster can and does consume!

Installing MySQL-Max

There are several different methods of obtaining MySQL:

- Install a binary package, either using some sort of formal package or just a tar file.
- Compile from source, using a package of source code.
- Download the latest nightly build and compile from that, using BitKeeper.

The easiest method is to install a binary package with precompiled executables and libraries and that does not require any configuration to work. All the files will be placed in whatever the maker of the package considers the "standard" location. The binaries can come in RPM or other package such as a Mac OS X package (either directly from MySQL.com or from your Linux/UNIX distributor, such as Red Hat) or as a tarball that you can download from MySQL.com. There is a significant distinction between these two methods: The tarball puts all the files in one folder (if you follow the guide in the manual, it is /usr/local/mysql). The RPM package, however, does not put all the files in one folder, but spreads them out according to where you get the binary from. This can lead to confusion, so if you install binaries from someone other than MySQL.com, you should make sure to spend some time familiarizing yourself with any different locations for files.

> **Note**
> You should ensure that you get the MySQL-Max release and not the regular distribution. The -Max designation means that the compilation has extra features compared to the regular distribution. One such feature is enabling support for MySQL Cluster, which you definitely need if you want to set up such a cluster!

The second, and far less common and more complex, method of installing MySQL-Max is to compile from source. There are many valid reasons to do this, but for the sake of performance and sanity, we recommend that you do not compile from source if possible but instead use a precompiled binary package. Furthermore, we suggest that if possible, you use a binary package provided by MySQL rather than your Linux distributor. If you ever want support—either paid-for support from MySQL or just helpful people on the mailing lists—you will find it much easier to get help if you have all your files in the place that MySQL decided to put them rather than wherever your distribution provider decided to put them. For example, in this book we assume that my.cnf is in the /etc/ folder. On Debian binary installations, it is actually in /etc/mysql/, which may well cause confusion, particularly for users fairly new to Linux or a particular distribution. Another reason to avoid third-party binaries is that most of their distributions do not include support for MySQL Cluster. A final reason to use the packages provided by MySQL is that you know that you can always access the latest version; you also do not rely on someone else to produce a package, which may take time.

Although we recommend that you install MySQL using the binary tarball available from MySQL.com, this chapter briefly covers installing MySQL using all common methods. In this book, we use CentOS 4.0, which is identical (except for branding) to Red Hat Enterprise Linux 4 and is a good choice if you want a solid Linux distribution without any formal support; however, you should find that these steps work correctly on all common Linux distributions.

This chapter also covers installing the latest nightly release from BitKeeper. You should not do this unless you hit a bug that is not fixed in a regular release but that has been fixed by a developer and will be in the nightly build. (BitKeeper is really just the "cutting edge" source code and includes lots of code that is new or has changed since the last formal release.) We include this information here simply because there are few clear guides available on this topic, yet installing BitKeeper is not particularly difficult to do. We strongly recommend that you never use code from BitKeeper in a production environment because it has not been tested as much (or at all, in some cases) as a full release.

Note that if you are running SELinux (Security Enhanced Linux), you should either create a new policy or disable it. Creating policies is beyond the scope of this book, but basically, to disable it, you edit the file /etc/sysconfig/selinux, change/add the SELINUX=disabled line, and reboot the system. If you want to leave SELinux enabled, visit the website for this book to download a rule that will allow you to run a MySQL cluster with SELinux.

All the examples in this book are for MySQL Cluster version 5.0, which we expect will be the generally available release by the time that this book is published. However, the steps are virtually identical for versions 4.1 and 5.1.

Installing MySQL Cluster from a Binary Tarball

To install MySQL Cluster from a binary tarball, you need to locate the correct tarball for your platform at the MySQL download page (for version 5.0, this is http://dev.mysql.com/downloads/mysql/5.0.html) and then obtain the relevant file. You then need to extract it, move it to the correct folder, add the mysql user, set up the initial tables, and start the server:

```
[user@host] su -
[root@host] cd /usr/local/
[root@host] wget <url-of-mirror>/mysql-max-5.0.11-beta-linux-i686.tar.gz
[root@host] tar -zxvf mysql-max-5.0.11-beta-linux-i686.tar.gz
[root@host] rm -f mysql-max-5.0.11-beta-linux-i686.tar.gz
[root@host] ls
bin   games    lib      mysql-max-5.0.12-beta-linux-i686   share
etc   include  libexec  sbin                               src
```

Note that a folder is created, with the "full" name of the distribution (*mysql-max-5.0.12-beta-linux-i686*, in the preceding example). For the sake of neatness and upgradeability, you should create a soft link (that is, a symlink) to this folder mysql. This also helps with upgrading because you can install both the older and new versions and then just stop MySQL, change the link, and start the upgraded version very easily. You can create this link easily:

```
[root@host] ln -s mysql-max-5.0.11-beta-linux-i686 mysql
[root@host] cd mysql
```

The MySQL database server can run as either root or any other user on the system. From a security point of view, it's a bad idea (and the developers have made it quite difficult) to run the MySQL database server as root; therefore, you should create a special mysql user and group for this purpose:

```
[root@host] groupadd mysql
[root@host] useradd -g mysql mysql
```

Now you need to tell MySQL where you want it to store its data. Unless you want it to store the databases in the same folder as the actual programs (/usr/local/mysql/data/), you should create a file called /etc/my.cnf that has the following contents:

> **Note**
> Storing the databases in the same folder as the actual programs is probably a bad idea. It is almost always a good idea to keep your data (databases) far away from your applications (binaries). This makes upgrading much easier, and it reduces the chance of a botched upgrade or installation destroying your data. If you choose not to follow this advice, you should change the second chown command to change the permissions on the folder /usr/local/mysql/data.

```
[mysqld]
datadir=/var/lib/mysql
socket=/var/lib/mysql/mysql.sock
[mysqld_safe]
err-log=/var/log/mysqld.log
pid-file=/var/run/mysqld/mysqld.pid
```

Next, you need to initialize the system database and tables. This means creating the mysql and test databases as well as the system tables that MySQL needs in order to run. You must also make sure that these new tables are owned by the mysql user:

```
[root@host] mkdir /var/lib/mysql
[root@host] /usr/local/mysql/scripts/mysql_install_db
[root@host] chown -R root:mysql /usr/local/mysql
[root@host] chown -R mysql:mysql /var/lib/mysql
```

On distributions of Linux that support the *service servicename* start command and syntax, you should copy the helpful mysql.server script into the /etc/rc.d/init.d/ folder (where the service command can find it):

```
[root@host] cp /usr/local/mysql/support-files/mysql.server /etc/rc.d/init.d/mysql
[root@host] service mysql start
```

Otherwise, you should copy the mysql server to wherever your distribution keeps init scripts and execute it.

You now need to add the MySQL bin directory to the PATH variable so you do not need to append /usr/local/mysql/bin/ before each binary name every time you want to use it. If you use the BASH shell, as most distributions do, you need to edit your .bash_profile file in your home directory. You need to make sure to change this file for each user on the system. Essentially, this involves opening up $HOME/.bash_profile with a text editor (such as vi/vim, pico, or emacs) and adding /usr/local/mysql/bin to the line that defines the variable $PATH, which may look something like this:

```
PATH=$PATH:$HOME/bin
```

You change it to this:

```
PATH=$PATH:$HOME/bin:/usr/local/mysql/bin
```

Then you log out and log back in again. The quickest way to test whether it is all working is to try to run the MySQL client:

```
[root@host] mysql -V
mysql  Ver 14.12 Distrib 5.0.11-beta, for pc-linux-gnu (i686) using readline 5.
```

If you get an error such as -bash: mysql: command not found, you have not correctly changed the path. If you get the correct version, you have MySQL-Max installed.

There are many other things you would need to do if you were installing a server in a production environment (for example, set a root password, optimize my.cnf), but we do not cover these steps here. If you are not entirely confident with any of these things, you should consult the MySQL manual.

Upgrading a Binary Tarball Setup

To upgrade a binary tarball setup, you follow this process:

1. Download the new .tar.gz file in /usr/local/ and then extract it.
2. Make a full backup.
3. Remove the symlink mysql.
4. Create a new symlink that points to the new full folder name.
5. Change the permissions on the new folder.
6. Restart MySQL.

You can see that this is very easy, and you can also see how easy it is to switch back: All you need to do is replace the mysql symlink with the old one and restart MySQL.

You should also be able to see why we recommend that you not have your data directory in the same place as your binaries. If you do, you need to copy the original data directory over to the new data directory and reset the permissions on it.

Installing from a Binary RPM

Installing from a binary RPM is the easiest method of installing MySQL-Max. Essentially, all you need to do is download and install the RPMs you need. Table 1.1 lists the RPMs you need for each node.

TABLE 1.1   The RPM Packages Provided by MySQL

Package	Description	SQL	Storage	Management
MySQL-server	The basic MySQL server	Yes	No	No
MySQL-Max	The extra packages that convert MySQL-standard to MySQL-Max	Yes	No	No
MySQL-client	The MySQL client program	Yes	No	No
MySQL-devel	Libraries and header files	Probably	No	No
MySQL-shared	Dynamic client libraries	Probably	No	No
MySQL-bench	Benchmarking tools	Up to you	No	No
MySQL-ndb-storage	Storage node binaries	No	Yes	No
MySQL-ndb-tools	Storage node tools	No	Yes[1]	No
MySQL-ndb-extra	Extra storage node tools	No	Yes	No
MySQL-ndb-management	Management node tools	No	No	Yes

1. You don't strictly need this or the MySQL-ndb-extra package to run a storage node, but we strongly recommend that you install it because this book often uses packages that appear in all three storage node packages.

Running multiple nodes on one machine is absolutely fine: You just need to install all the packages you might need. For example, to run a storage and SQL node on a server (but not a management node), you should install MySQL-server, MySQL-ndb-storage, MySQL-ndb-tools, MySQL-ndb-extra, and MySQL-Max.

The actual installation process is as simple as obtaining the RPMs you need and installing them. To install all the packages (for SQL, storage, and management nodes as well as benchmarking tools), you use the following commands. Note that this is the process for RPM packages; however, you can easily change this to suit other forms of package, such as those found on OS X. First of all, you obtain the packages:

```
[user@host] su -
[root@host] cd /tmp/
```

```
[root@host] rm -f MySQL-*-5.0.11-0.i386.rpm
[root@host] wget <url-of-mirror>/MySQL-Max-5.0.11-0.i386.rpm
[root@host] wget <url-of-mirror>/MySQL-bench-5.0.11-0.i386.rpm
[root@host] wget <url-of-mirror>/MySQL-client-5.0.11-0.i386.rpm
[root@host] wget <url-of-mirror>/MySQL-devel-5.0.11-0.i386.rpm
[root@host] wget <url-of-mirror>/MySQL-ndb-storage-5.0.11-0.i386.rpm
[root@host] wget <url-of-mirror>/MySQL-ndb-management-5.0.11-0.i386.rpm
[root@host] wget <url-of-mirror>/MySQL-ndb-tools-5.0.11-0.i386.rpm
[root@host] wget <url-of-mirror>/MySQL-ndb-extra-5.0.11-0.i386.rpm
```

Then you install them. For RPMs, this should be as simple as using the following command:

```
[root@host] rpm -i MySQL-*-5.0.11-0.i386.rpm
```

This installs MySQL with every optional extra package. You should be aware that the benchmarking tools require perl-DBI, which you may have to obtain before you can install the RPM.

Upgrading a Binary RPM Setup

To upgrade an RPM setup, you simply download the new RPMs, stop MySQL, and run the following command on each RPM:

```
rpm -U MySQL-whatever-version.i386.rpm
```

An issue you may have if you completely remove and reinstall MySQL (that is, if you run rpm -e before installing the new RPM) is that if you have the "cluster lines" that are discussed shortly in the [mysqld] section of /etc/my.cnf file (for example, ndb-connectstring), the commands shown here will fail because the package manager will attempt to restart MySQL after installing the standard MySQL server before it installs MySQL-Max. Without MySQL-Max, you cannot have cluster commands in my.cnf (it throws an error because it has no idea what to do with the parameters), so MySQL will fail to start. The solution is to comment out the offending lines in my.cnf or move my.cnf somewhere else during the upgrade. As soon as all the packages are installed, you can go back to your existing my.cnf.

Compiling from Source

Remember that unless you have a really good reason to install MySQL Cluster by compiling from source, it is probably a bad idea. However, if for some reason you want to compile your own copy, this section provides the steps you should follow. You need GNU bison 1.75 (or newer), make, autoconf 2.58 (or newer), automake 1.8, libtool 1.5, and m4 to run the next set of commands. Even though many operating systems come with their own implementations of make, chances are good that the compilation will fail with strange error messages if you use their versions; therefore, it is highly recommended that you use GNU make (sometimes called gmake) instead.

First, you need to download the source tarball from MySQL.com:

```
[user@host] su -
[root@host] cd /tmp/
[root@host] wget <url-of-mirror>/mysql-5.0.11-beta.tar.gz
[root@host] tar -zxvf mysql-5.0.11-beta.tar.gz
[root@host] cd  mysql-5.0.11-beta
```

When you have obtained the source code, it is time to compile it. At this stage, you can issue whatever flags you want to the compiler in addition to the basic ones listed here:

```
[root@host] ./configure --prefix=/usr/local/mysql -with-ndbcluster
[root@host] make
[root@host] make test
[root@host] make install
[root@host] groupadd mysql
[root@host] useradd -g mysql mysql
```

You then install MySQL and add the mysql user and group.

Now you need to tell MySQL where you want it to store its data. Unless you want it to store the databases in a subdirectory in the same folder as the actual programs (/usr/local/mysql/var), you should create the file /etc/my.cnf, with the following contents:

> **Note**
> Remember that it is safest not to store databases in the same folder as the actual programs.

```
[mysqld]
datadir=/var/lib/mysql
socket=/var/lib/mysql/mysql.sock

[mysqld_safe]
err-log=/var/log/mysqld.log
pid-file=/var/run/mysqld/mysqld.pid
```

Next, you need to initialize the tables. This means you need to create the system databases that MySQL needs to run. You should then make sure that these new tables are owned by the mysql user:

```
[root@host] /usr/local/mysql/bin/mysql_install_db
[root@host] chown -R root:mysql /usr/local/mysql
[root@host] chown -R mysql:mysql /var/lib/mysql
```

You should now have a working MySQL installation, which you can start like this:

```
[root@host] /usr/local/mysql/bin/mysqld_safe --user=mysql &
```

> **Note**
> As described earlier in this chapter in the section "Installing MySQL Cluster from a Binary
> Tarball," you should install the `mysql.server` script and add the MySQL `bin` directory to the
> `$PATH` variable, but in this case, you find the `mysql.server` script in the
> `/usr/local/mysql/share/mysql/` folder (not in the `support.files` folder).

Upgrading a Source Installation

To upgrade a source installation, you simply carry out the preceding steps, from `su-` through `make install`, but you stop MySQL first and start it again after the installation is complete.

Retrieving the Latest Snapshot from BitKeeper

BitKeeper is a commercial revision control system that MySQL uses to manage its massive amount of code and control updates. There may be situations in which you want the latest version of the code, and this is how to get it.

First, you need to install the BitKeeper client. You need to have `zlib` installed before you attempt to install BitKeeper (which may involve installing both the `zlib` and `zlib-devel` packages). When you have `zlib`, you need to download and install the BitKeeper client. This can be achieved with the following commands:

```
[alex@host]$ su -
Password:
[root@host]# cd /tmp/
[root@host]# wget http://www.bitmover.com/bk-client.shar
--00:31:15--  http://www.bitmover.com/bk-client.shar
           => `bk-client.shar'
Resolving www.bitmover.com... 192.132.92.2
Connecting to www.bitmover.com[192.132.92.2]:80... connected.
HTTP request sent, awaiting response... 200 OK
Length: 28,867 [application/x-shar]

100%[====================================>] 28,867        123.59K/s

00:31:16 (123.15 KB/s) - `bk-client.shar' saved [28,867/28,867]

[root@host]# sh bk-client.shar
x - creating lock directory
x - creating directory bk_client-1.1
x - extracting bk_client-1.1/demo.sh (text)
x - extracting bk_client-1.1/Makefile (text)
```

```
x - extracting bk_client-1.1/update.c (text)
x - extracting bk_client-1.1/sfioball.c (text)
x - extracting bk_client-1.1/sfio.c (text)
x - extracting bk_client-1.1/system.h (text)
[root@host]# cd bk_client-1.1/
[root@host]# make all
cc -O2 -o sfio -lz sfio.c
cc -O2    sfioball.c   -o sfioball
cc -O2    update.c   -o update
[root@host]# PATH=$PWD:$PATH
```

Now you need to download the latest copy of the source:

```
[root@host bk_client-1.1]# mkdir /usr/src/mysql
[root@host bk_client-1.1]# cd /usr/src/mysql
[root@host mysql]# sfioball bk://mysql.bkbits.net/mysql-5.0 5.0
OK-root OK
```

(More output appears as the latest source is retrieved.)

Next, you need to compile and install the code. You need GNU bison 1.75 (or newer), make, autoconf 2.58 (or newer), automake 1.8, libtool 1.5, and m4 to run the next set of commands. Even though many operating systems come with their own implementations of make, chances are good that the compilation will fail with strange error messages if you use their versions; therefore, it is highly recommended that you use GNU make (sometimes called gmake) instead.

The commands for compiling and installing the source code follow:

```
[root@host] cd 5.0
[root@host] bk -r edit
[root@host] aclocal; autoheader
[root@host] libtoolize --automake --force
[root@host] automake --force --add-missing; autoconf
[root@host] (cd innobase; aclocal; autoheader; autoconf; automake)
[root@host] (cd bdb/dist; sh s_all)
[root@host] ./configure --prefix=/usr/local/mysql -with-ndbcluster
[root@host] make
[root@host] BUILD/autorun.sh
```

If you get some strange errors at this stage, you should verify that you really have libtool installed. Otherwise, when the build is done, you should run make install. You need to be careful with this on a production machine because the command may overwrite your live release installation. If you have another installation of MySQL, you should run ./configure with different values for the --prefix, --with-tcp-port, and --unix-socket-path options than those used for your production server so your new source install runs in parallel and does not interfere with your production version. Of course, if you have the resources, it is highly recommended that you do your testing on non-production machines.

> **Note**
> Another way you can get a recent version of the source code, without needing BitKeeper or the automake toolchain, is to visit http://downloads.mysql.com. MySQL AB publishes nightly source code snapshots that are available for download at that location. These snapshots do the preceding steps for you and give you a version of the code that you can install exactly the same way you do the regular source code.

Upgrading a BitKeeper Installation

If you want to update the BitKeeper code any time after you first install it, you simply run these commands:

```
[alex@host]$ su -
Password:
[root@host]# cd /usr/src/mysql/
[root@host]# update bk://mysql.bkbits.net/mysql-5.0 5.0
```

Then you continue with the following commands:

```
[root@host] cd 5.0
[root@host] bk -r edit
[root@host] aclocal; autoheader
[root@host] libtoolize --automake --force
[root@host] automake --force --add-missing; autoconf
[root@host] (cd innobase; aclocal; autoheader; autoconf; automake)
[root@host] (cd bdb/dist; sh s_all)
[root@host] ./configure --prefix=/usr/local/mysql -with-ndbcluster
[root@host] make
[root@host] BUILD/autorun.sh
```

Ensuring That MySQL Cluster Works

On all your nodes, you should now check that you have indeed installed support for MySQL Cluster, whether you have installed from a binary or compiled from source. To do this, you issue a SHOW TABLE TYPES command in the MySQL client:

```
[root@host]# mysql
mysql> show storage engines;
+------------+--------+-------------------------------------------------------
| Engine     | Support | Comment
+------------+--------+-------------------------------------------------------
| MyISAM     | DEFAULT | Default engine as of MySQL 3.23 with great performance
| MEMORY     | YES     | Hash based, stored in memory, useful for temporary tables
| HEAP       | YES     | Alias for MEMORY
```

```
| MERGE      | YES     | Collection of identical MyISAM tables
| MRG_MYISAM | YES     | Alias for MERGE
| ISAM       | NO      | Obsolete storage engine, now replaced by MyISAM
| MRG_ISAM   | NO      | Obsolete storage engine, now replaced by MERGE
| InnoDB     | YES     | Supports transactions, row-level locking, and foreign key
| INNOBASE   | YES     | Alias for INNODB
| BDB        | YES     | Supports transactions and page-level locking
| BERKELEYDB | YES     | Alias for BDB
| NDBCLUSTER | DISABLED| Clustered, fault-tolerant, memory-based tables
| NDB        | YES     | Alias for NDBCLUSTER
| EXAMPLE    | YES     | Example storage engine
| ARCHIVE    | YES     | Archive storage engine
| CSV        | YES     | CSV storage engine
| FEDERATED  | YES     | Federated MySQL storage engine
| BLACKHOLE  | YES     | /dev/null storage engine (anything you write to it disapp
+------------+--------+--------------------------------------------------------
18 rows in set, 1 warning (0.00 sec)
```

If you have the words NDBCLUSTER and YES or DISABLED on the same line, you are done, and you can continue with the process described in the next section. Otherwise, you need to go back and try to determine what you did wrong: Either you failed to install the MySQL-Max binary, or you failed to add support for ndbcluster in your compile string.

Configuring and Starting a Cluster

After you have installed the relevant packages on each node in your cluster, you need to log in to the server on which you are going to run your management node and start to define your cluster.

First, you need to check whether the directory /var/lib/mysql-cluster exists, and if it does not, you need to create it. Within it, using your favorite text editor, you create a file called config.ini in which you define the nodes in your cluster (this is where all settings go for all nodes). All the other nodes need is a one-line configuration line called a connect string, which goes in my.cnf and tells the nodes where they can find the management node.

You should be aware that you can put config.ini wherever you like. What matters is that when you start the management daemon, you must be in the folder that contains config.ini. Some people therefore put it in /etc/. You still need to create the directory /var/lib/mysql-cluster, which your nodes will use to store data that they need to store to disk.

You can also define your settings within config.ini in my.cnf; however, this is not recommended if you want to keep your cluster configuration away from your database configuration, which in most cases is a good idea.

Editing `config.ini`

Let's start with the basics. A `config.ini` file is made up of different sections and looks exactly like a traditional Windows `.ini` file, with sections separated by titles in square brackets.

There are two separate parts to a `config.ini` file. First, you define defaults and settings across the cluster in the following sections:

- `[NDBD DEFAULT]` contains defaults for all storage nodes.
- `[TCP DEFAULT]` contains networking settings for all nodes (ports and so on).
- `[MYSQLD DEFAULT]` contains defaults for all SQL nodes.
- `[NDB_MGMD DEFAULT]` contains defaults for all management nodes (typically, you only have one management node, so this is rather pointless).

Then you specify the settings for each particular node, with one section per node:

```
[NDB_MGMD] Management node
[NDBD] Storage node
[MYSQLD] SQL node
```

You'll learn all the different options that you can put in each section in Chapter 2, "Configuration." At this point, we look at the settings you must define to get your cluster working. Next, we cover each section of the `config.ini` file.

[NDBD_DEFAULT]

`NoOfReplicas` defines the number of copies of each piece of data the cluster will hold. Clearly, if you want redundancy, `NoOfReplicas` must be greater than or equal to 2. If you have a fixed number of storage nodes, it is worth remembering your total number of storage nodes should be a power of 2 and a multiple of `NoOfReplicas`—so if you set `NoOfReplicas` to 2, you should have 2, 4, or 8 (and so on) storage nodes. This is a not mandatory (your cluster will still work if you don't) but will gain you significant increases in performance due to the method of partitioning that the current versions of MySQL Cluster (4.1 and 5.0) use. It is expected that this will become less important in MySQL Cluster 5.1. Note that there is an exception: If `NumberOfReplicas` is equal to the total number of storage nodes, that is fine (even if the total number of storage nodes is not a power of 2).

`NoOfReplicas` also specifies the size of node groups. A *node group* is a set of nodes that all store the same information. Node groups are formed implicitly. The first node group is formed by the set of data nodes with the lowest node IDs, the next node group by the set of the next-lowest node identities, and so on. It is important to configure the cluster in such a manner that nodes in the same node groups are not placed on the same computer. (You will see how to do this in the next section.) In this situation, a single hardware failure would cause the entire cluster to crash. (This book's introduction provides a graphical illustration and further description of this concept.)

DataDir defines the folder that the node will use when it flushes its data to disk. This data on disk is used to recover from a cluster crash where no node in one or more node groups is left alive. We strongly suggest that you set this to /var/lib/mysql-cluster.

[NDB_MGMD] (Management), [NDBD] (Storage), and [MYSQLD] (SQL)

You must define at least one management node, one SQL node, and two storage nodes in order for your cluster to work. All three of the sections [NDB_MGMD], [NDBD], and [MYSQLD] require the parameter Hostname, which defines either the hostname or the IP address of the node. We strongly suggest that you use IP addresses, and when troubleshooting, you should certainly use IP addresses. Many problems are caused by using hostnames unless both the forward and reverse DNS are in perfect order, which on many hosts they are not. If you use hostnames, you should try to define them in /etc/hosts to reduce your reliance on DNS lookups.

An Example of a config.ini File

If you have three separate servers and want to run storage nodes on two of them, SQL nodes on all three, and the management node on the server that does not have a storage node, you produce a configuration like this, where 10.0.0.1, 10.0.0.2, and 10.0.0.3 are the IP addresses of the servers:

```
[NDBD DEFAULT]
NoOfReplicas=2
DataDir= /var/lib/mysql-cluster
# Management Node
[NDB_MGMD]
HostName=10.0.0.1
DataDir= /var/lib/mysql-cluster

# Storage Nodes
# One entry for each node
[NDBD]
HostName=10.0.0.2
[NDBD]
HostName=10.0.0.3

# SQL Nodes
# One entry for each node
[MYSQLD]
HostName=10.0.0.1
[MYSQLD]
HostName=10.0.0.2
[MYSQLD]
HostName=10.0.0.3
```

We use this sample configuration for the rest of this chapter, and if you are able to get your hands on three servers, we strongly recommend that you start out using this configuration.

> **Note**
>
> We use the same three IP addresses for the rest of this chapter, so if you have different ones on your servers, we recommend that you now write down a list of the IP addresses in the book (10.0.0.1, 10.0.0.2, and 10.0.0.3) and the IP addresses of your servers. You can then just substitute the former for the latter each time that you want to try something.
>
> Of course, if you do have three completely spare servers, you can actually set their IP addresses to 10.0.0.1, 10.0.0.2, and 10.0.0.3, and then you will avoid any chance of confusion when following the examples in this book.

You should now be able to produce a simple cluster with a slightly different format than shown in the preceding example—perhaps with three replicas and three storage nodes[2] or two replicas and four storage nodes. However you want to set up your first cluster, write out your `config.ini` file and check it before advancing to the next step.

You only need to define ID if you are planning on running multiple storage nodes on the same physical machines. If you do not define this parameter, the management daemon will assign IDs in the order in which they connect.

If you define IDs for storage nodes, it is good practice to also define an ID for the management node, typically 1. You do this by including an ID line in the [NDB_MGMD] section.

You can choose a number between 1 and 64 for this parameter; node groups are formed from consecutive IDs, so if you have four storage nodes and `NumberOfReplicas` is equal to 2 (that is, each node group contains two nodes), the first two IDs will form Node Group 1, and the second two will form Node Group 2.

If you have two physical servers, you need to make sure that you define the IDs such that storage nodes on the same physical machine are in different node groups, as in this example:

```
Server 1, First Storage node: ID # 2 (nodegroup 1)
Server 1, Second Storage node: ID # 4 (nodegroup 2)
Server 2, First Storage node: ID # 3 (nodegroup 1)
Server 2, Second Storage node: ID # 5 (nodegroup 2)
```

This means that Server 1 has a node in both node groups on it, which is good because each node group holds only 50% of the data, so you need members of both node groups to actually have a complete set of data in the cluster. This means that a failure of either server does not remove all nodes in one node group, so your cluster can survive.

---

2. All you would have to do in this example is change **NumberOfReplicass** to 3 and add another [NDBD] section with **HostName=10.0.0.1** in it.

Starting a Management Node

You now need to start the *management daemon*. This is the program that runs in the background and controls your cluster.

To start the management daemon, you log in as root to the server you want to run your management node, change directory to /var/lib/mysql-cluster, and start the ndb_mgmd daemon:

```
[user@mgm] su -
[root@mgm] cd /var/lib/mysql-cluster
[root@mgm] ndb_mgmd
```

Alternatively, you can start the ndb_mgmd daemon from any folder and pass the location of the configuration file to the daemon:

```
[root@mgm] ndb_mgmd -f /var/lib/mysql-cluster/config.ini
```

Note that this example assumes that you have the MySQL bin directory in your path; if you do not, you need to add /usr/local/mysql/bin/ (or wherever you installed your binaries) in front of ndb_mgmd and in front of every other MySQL binary in this book. Refer to the end of section "Installing MySQL Cluster from a Binary Tarball," earlier in this chapter, for instructions on how to add to your path.

If the output from the ndb_mgmd daemon is nothing at all, you are okay. If you get an error, you almost certainly made a mistake in your config.ini file, so you need to go back and compare it with the preceding example, and if you are still stuck, refer to Chapter 2, which explains exactly what to put where in a config.ini file.

The next step is to enter the management console, which is the client to the management node—rather like the mysql binary is a client to the MySQL server. The management console is called ndb_mgm. You log in to the management node and issue the command SHOW, which asks the management daemon to send it details about the current status of the cluster:

```
[user@mgm] ndb_mgm
-- NDB Cluster -- Management Client --
ndb_mgm> SHOW
Connected to Management Server at: 10.0.0.1:1186
Cluster Configuration
---------------------
[ndbd(NDB)]     2 node(s)
id=2 (not connected, accepting connect from 10.0.0.2)
id=3 (not connected, accepting connect from 10.0.0.3)

[ndb_mgmd(MGM)] 1 node(s)
id=1    @10.0.0.1 (Version: 5.0.11)
```

```
[mysqld(API)]   3 node(s)
id=4 (not connected, accepting connect from 10.0.0.1)
id=5 (not connected, accepting connect from 10.0.0.2)
id=6 (not connected, accepting connect from 10.0.0.3)
```

If, on the other hand, you get an error like this when you attempt to use SHOW, your management daemon has failed to start properly:

```
ndb_mgm> SHOW
Unable to connect with connect string: nodeid=0,127.0.0.1:1186
```

If this is what you get, you should turn to Chapter 6, "Troubleshooting," for ideas on solving this sort of issue.

Starting Storage Nodes

In order to get your cluster to work, you need to connect your storage nodes. The process is identical on all storage nodes, so you can complete it with one and then repeat the same process for all your other storage nodes. Essentially, all you need to do is tell the daemon where to find the management server and then start the ndbd daemon (which is the storage daemon).

To tell the daemon where to find the management server, you can either put some lines in /etc/my.cnf or you can pass it as a command-line parameter. We suggest that you use my.cnf, but we illustrate both methods here. Note that it is not a bad idea to add these lines to /etc/my.cnf on the management server as well, even if it is not acting as a storage node. If you do not, it will just connect to the local machine (127.0.0.1), which normally works (we relied on it working earlier), but when it becomes possible to bind the management daemon to one IP address, you may no longer be able to rely on it working without an IP address (even if it is just the primary IP of the local machine) in my.cnf.

To use my.cnf, you create the file /etc/my.cnf, if it does not already exist, and add the following:

```
[mysql_cluster]
ndb-connectstring=10.0.0.1
```

Then you need to start the storage node daemon, ndbd:

```
[root@storage] ndbd --initial
```

This should return no output if it works.

The other way to do it does not involve a my.cnf file. When you start ndbd, you just pass the connect string to it, like this:

```
[root@storage] ndbd --connect-string=10.0.0.1 --initial
```

The only way to tell if this method works is to return to the management console (by using ndb_mgm on the management server) and see if the status has changed. If you do this after starting one storage node, you get output like this:

```
ndb_mgm> SHOW
Cluster Configuration
---------------------
[ndbd(NDB)]     2 node(s)
id=2 (not connected, accepting connect from 10.0.0.2)
id=3   @10.0.0.3  (Version: 5.0.10, starting, Nodegroup: 0, Master)
```

If it has not changed and you still get all lines reporting "not connected," then something has gone wrong. Refer to Chapter 6 for further help.

When you have all your storage nodes started, you should see that the output from SHOW in ndb_mgm changes to Started:

```
ndb_mgm> SHOW
Cluster Configuration
---------------------
[ndbd(NDB)]     2 node(s)
id=2   @10.0.0.2  (Version: 5.0.11, Nodegroup: 0, Master)
id=3   @10.0.0.3  (Version: 5.0.11, Nodegroup: 0)

[ndb_mgmd(MGM)] 1 node(s)
id=1   @10.0.0.1  (Version: 5.0.11)
```

This means that your cluster is working. However, you need to connect at least one SQL node before you can start using it.

Connecting SQL Nodes

The requirement for a SQL node is that it must have MySQL-Max rather than just MySQL. Apart from that, you can use any recent version of MySQL to connect to your new cluster. All you need to do is add two lines to the [mysqld] section of my.cnf:

```
[mysqld]
ndbcluster
ndb-connectstring=10.0.0.1
```

In this example, 10.0.0.1 is the IP address or hostname (not recommended) of your management node.

You then simply have to restart MySQL, with a command such as service mysql restart.

If MySQL fails to come up, you should check the error log—typically /var/lib/mysql/hostname.err. If you have an error such as the following:

```
[ERROR] /usr/sbin/mysqld: unknown variable 'ndb-connectstring=10.0.0.1'
```

you do not have the MySQL-Max package installed or you did not include support for NDB during your compilation process if you compiled from source. Refer to the earlier section in this chapter "Installing MySQL-Max" for further advice.

An Example of a Working Cluster

If you have created the config.ini file described in this chapter, with three servers and two storage nodes, one management node, and three SQL nodes, you should get the following output from a SHOW command:

```
[user@mgm]# ndb_mgm
-- NDB Cluster -- Management Client --
ndb_mgm> SHOW
Connected to Management Server at: 10.0.0.1:1186
Cluster Configuration
---------------------
[ndbd(NDB)]     2 node(s)
id=2    @10.0.0.2  (Version: 5.0.11, Nodegroup: 0, Master)
id=3    @10.0.0.3  (Version: 5.0.11, Nodegroup: 0)

[ndb_mgmd(MGM)] 1 node(s)
id=1    @10.0.0.1  (Version: 5.0.11)

[mysqld(API)]   3 node(s)
id=4    @10.0.0.1  (Version: 5.0.11)
id=5    @10.0.0.2  (Version: 5.0.11)
id=6    @10.0.0.3  (Version: 5.0.11)
```

Notice how the storage nodes (called "NDB nodes" in the management client) have a Nodegroup parameter. Both storage nodes are in Node Group 0; you should have been expecting this because you have NumberOfReplicas defined as two, and you have two storage nodes; therefore, you have one node group. If you added another two storage nodes, you would have two node groups.

Creating a Table

Now that you have MySQL Cluster working, you can start to create some tables. To do so, you log in to the MySQL client on any one of the SQL nodes (using your mysql root user and password if you have created one), and then you create a database and table and insert and select a row:

```
[user@any]# mysql
mysql> create database clustertest;
Query OK, 1 row affected (0.03 sec)
```

```
mysql> use clustertest;
Database changed
mysql> create table ctest (i INT) ENGINE = NDBCLUSTER;
Query OK, 0 rows affected (4.27 sec)

mysql> INSERT into ctest () VALUES (1);
Query OK, 1 row affected (0.63 sec)

mysql> SELECT i from ctest;
+------+
| i    |
+------+
|    1 |
+------+
1 row in set (0.05 sec)
```

You can see that this has all worked. If the cluster is not actually working properly, you may get an error such as ERROR 1015 (HY000): Can't lock file (errno: 4009) or ERROR 1050 (42S01): Table 'ctest' already exists while attempting to create the table or while selecting or inserting the row. In this case, you need to go back to ndb_mgm and ensure that all nodes in the cluster are correctly started, referring to Chapter 6 for help, if needed.

The final thing you are likely to want to check is that all your SQL nodes are actually working, so if you insert one row on one node, it does appear on all the others. You can do this by logging in to each storage node and inserting another row before selecting all rows. However, before you try to do this, you should read the next section on auto-discovery of databases.

Auto-discovery of Databases

MySQL Cluster does not currently feature auto-discovery of databases on SQL nodes, so you have to manually create each database on each SQL node before MySQL Cluster will start to show the tables. You can create the database on some SQL nodes after you have actually created the database on another SQL node and created the table; you can consider using the create database command as a way of saying "go look for my cluster tables in this database." You should also run FLUSH TABLES after you have completed the database to make sure the SQL node picks up the tables. You do *not* need to create tables on each SQL node. MySQL features auto-discovery of tables, so you simply need to create each database on each SQL node.

If you drop a database, you will delete the tables within it from all the storage nodes. So be careful; you can't just drop the database and expect it to remain on other nodes!

Startup Phases

While your storage nodes are starting up, you can get slightly more detailed information about what they are doing via the management client.

If you enter *<id>* STATUS, the management client will tell you what phase of the startup process you are in, as in this example:

```
ndb_mgm> 2 STATUS
Node 2: starting (Phase 2) (Version 5.0.11)

ndb_mgm> 2 STATUS
Node 2: started (Version 5.0.11)
```

You can also use the ALL STATUS command to list the status for all nodes at the same time.

A quick description of what the cluster is doing during each phase follows; this is often useful when you are debugging problems as it gives you a hint as to exactly what problems you are experiencing:

> **Note**
> Note that some concepts here have not been explained in detail yet; they are intended to help you troubleshoot your problems, but if you do not have any problems yet or do not follow any of the points, feel free to skip this.

- Phase 1 is when the node first connects to all the other nodes in the cluster and heartbeats between nodes are initiated.
- Phase 2 is when an arbitrator is elected, if none exists.
- Phase 3 initializes the internal variables.
- Phase 4 finds the end of the logs and prepares for the node to start.
- Phase 5 copies the data from the alive nodes in the node group (if available) or starts the recovery from local checkpoints and the REDO log.
- Phase 6 and onward do various small other tidbits such as re-creating all ordered indexes, so you can expect high CPU usage.

Restarting a Cluster

To shut down a cluster cleanly, you issue the command SHUTDOWN in the management client and wait for all nodes to cleanly shut down. This will *not* shut down your SQL nodes—only your storage and management nodes. However, all tables you have converted to the NDB engine will not be available anymore because you have shut down all the storage nodes.

When you restart the storage nodes in your cluster (for example, by using the ndbd daemon), you should *not* use the --initial flag when you start ndbd. --initial simply means "I am running for the first time; please take DataDirectory, delete everything in it, and format it for my use." You use it in three situations:

- When starting the cluster for the first time
- When starting the cluster after making certain changes to config.ini (changes that affect the disk storage of the nodes—as discussed in Chapter 2)
- When upgrading the cluster to a new version

When you run ndbd with --initial, MySQL Cluster will clear the cluster file system. (This can be considered Stage 0 in the startup process.)

Note that starting all nodes in any one node group with the --initial flag at the same time after a shutdown will completely destroy all your data. The only time you should start all nodes with --initial is when you are installing it for the first time or when you are upgrading major versions and have very good backups.

Restarting on Failure

You will inevitably have to restart your cluster from time to time. We cover upgrading a cluster later on (see the section "Upgrading MySQL Cluster," later in this chapter), but here we describe how nodes resynchronize their data and cover the procedure to recover from the process of shutting down the complete cluster or just a single node.

How a Storage Node Stores Data to Disk

When a transaction (that is, a query) is committed, it is committed to the RAM in all nodes on which the data is mirrored. Transaction log records are *not* flushed to disk as part of the commit. This means that as long as one of the nodes remains working, the data is safe. It also means that there is no reading or writing to the disks during one transaction, which naturally removes that bottleneck.

However, of course this means that if all nodes suffer simultaneous failure that clears their RAM, you lose your data. Therefore, MySQL Cluster is designed to handle a complete cluster crash—that is, all nodes in any one node group (or all nodes) being killed (for example, if the power is cut to all servers and then any UPS system fails to work). It does this in several ways, all of which involve storing the data on the hard drives of the individual storage nodes in a process known as *check pointing*.

The first type of checkpoint, a global checkpoint, stores all the recent transactions in a log file format. The data node flushes the most recent REDO log (which contain all the recent transactions) to disk, which allows the cluster to reapply recent transactions in the event of total failure of all nodes in a node group. The frequency with which it updates this copy is controlled by the parameter TimeBetweenGlobalCheckpoints in config.ini and defaults to 2 seconds. Any less time, and you lose performance and increase durability; any greater time, and you lose durability and increase performance.

The second type of checkpoint, a local checkpoint (LCP), takes place on each storage node more or less concurrently. During an LCP, all the cluster's data is stored on the disk. In most clusters with high update rates, it is likely that a new LCP is started immediately after the previous one is completed; the default frequency is to start a new checkpoint after 4MB of write operations have built up since the last checkpoint was started. The LCP mechanism uses an UNDO log in order to allow it to create a completely consistent copy of the data without locking anything while doing so. An LCP is essentially the same process that occurs when you take an online backup with MySQL Cluster. The purpose of the LCP is to allow the data node to remove old REDO logs to prevent disk usage from always growing.

The cluster will store on disk the three most recent LCPs and the REDO logs for in between.

Single-Node Restart

If one node in each node group remains working, to start the other node(s) in the node group, you simply run ndbd on the servers where the dead node(s) reside, which should connect and start working.

In some situations, the data on the disk of a node can become corrupted, and if this is the case and the node fails to start properly, you simply start it with the --initial flag.

Doing an Entire Cluster Restart (System Restart)

If your entire cluster fails for some reason, the recovery can be more complicated than the recovery for a single node.

You should try to bring up your management node and then start to connect storage nodes. Each cluster node copies the last complete LCP it has on its disk back into RAM, and it then applies the latest complete global checkpoint (from the REDO log).

If none of these files are corrupted on any nodes, you should find that the startup is fairly quick and everything continues from where it was when it died.

However, if some nodes do not come up, you are still okay as long as one node in each node group has come up. You can start other nodes with ndbd --initial as long as there is another node in that node group that has started and has a complete set of data stored on it.

Note that normally a cluster doesn't want to start if not all the data nodes are connected. Therefore, the cluster waits longer during the restart if the nodes aren't all connected so that the other data nodes can connect. This period of time is specified in the setting StartPartialTimeout, which defaults to 30 seconds. If at the end of 30 seconds, a cluster is possible (that is, it has one node from each node group) and it can't be in a network partitioned situation (that is, it has all of one node group), the cluster will perform a partial cluster restart, in which it starts up even though data nodes are missing. If the cluster is in a potential network partitioned setup, where it doesn't have all of a single node group, then it will wait even longer, with a setting called StartPartitionedTimeout, which defaults to 60 seconds. Starting in this situation would be potentially dangerous because network partitioning can lead to data integrity issues. The reason for the extra wait is that a system restart is normally much faster than node restarts as it does not involve as much network traffic.

Testing Your Cluster

When your cluster is working and you understand how to restart nodes, it is time to ensure that it is indeed highly available. What you are now going to do is kill some nodes to make sure that the cluster remains working.

First of all, you open the MySQL client on one of the storage nodes and issue the SELECT query. Next, you go to the management node and either issue kill -9 to the ndb_mgmd process or, if the management node is alone on the server (in other words, if there is not a SQL or storage node also on the same server), unplug the network or power cable. Then you return to the SQL node (that is, the MySQL client) and issue the SELECT query, and you should find that it still works. If it does, you have just verified that your cluster can survive a failure of the management node. If you have more than one SQL node, you can try the query on all of them.

Next, you need to restart your management node. The procedure differs depending on how you killed the node:

- If you unplugged the power cable, you plug it back in and boot the machine and then follow the process for issuing kill -9.

- If you issued kill -9, all you need to do is repeat the previously described process above: change directory to /var/lib/mysql-cluster and start ndb_mgmd or use one of the other methods mentioned earlier.

- If you unplugged the network cable, all you need to do is plug it back in. Management nodes do not kill themselves after a certain period of time without communication (heartbeats) from other nodes as storage nodes do.

After you have restarted the management daemon by whatever means, you should run the management client, ndb_mgm, and issue a SHOW command to check that all the storage and SQL nodes have reconnected to the management server and that your cluster is back up and running. When you have established that all is well, you are ready to continue the testing.

You now want to establish whether your cluster is able to survive a failure of one of the storage nodes. In theory, your cluster can survive as long as one storage node in each node group remains alive. In the example we have been using so far in this chapter, there only is one node group, with two nodes in it, so you can only survive the failure of one storage node. If you had, for example, NumberOfReplicas set to 3 and had six storage nodes, you would be able to survive four nodes failing—two in each node group, although the cluster could potentially fail if three nodes failed (if they were all three nodes in one node group).

To check that your cluster is indeed highly available, you log in to a SQL node and run the MySQL client. You should then issue the SELECT query as before and verify that it works. Then you move over to the other storage node and either issue a kill -9 command for the ndbd process (there are actually two ndbd processes per node, so you need to kill both at the same time; otherwise, one can restart the other) or remove the power or network cable from the back of the server. (Again, this works only if the server is only running a storage node; if it is running a management node or the only SQL node, you should not do this!) You then repeat the SQL query on the surviving storage node, and you should find that it continues to work. If you issued a kill -9 command to kill the storage node on a server that also has a SQL node on it, the SQL node on that server should also continue to work, so you should test that as well.

Now you need to restart the storage node that you killed. If you reset the machine or killed the power and then powered the machine back on, you log in, su to root, and run ndbd. If you simply killed the ndbd process, you should be able just to start the ndbd process again.

If you removed the network cable, you should plug it back in and watch to see if the storage node attempts to connect to the management node (by looking at the output of SHOW in the ndb_mgm client). It will almost certainly not because ndbd will have exited previously. This is because the storage node will not have been able to contact the arbitrator (the management daemon) and will have killed itself. You should be aware that it is possible to cause the storage node not to shut down completely in the event of a network outage or similar situation, but instead to cause the node to attempt to reconnect periodically. For more information, you should read about the option StopOnError, which is covered in Chapter 2. In summary, if the ndbd (storage) node process has exited, you just start it again; if you were very quick, it might not have exited, and you might be able to just plug the cable back in again.

Upgrading MySQL Cluster

MySQL Cluster supports online upgrades within major releases. This means that you can upgrade from 5.0.10 to 5.0.11 without any downtime at all; however, you cannot upgrade from 4.1.x to 5.0.x without downtime.

Upgrading MySQL Cluster is very simple. The first thing you have to do is stop your current management node, upgrade it, and restart it. You then stop one storage node at a time, upgrade each, and start it up with the ndbd -initial command, waiting for it to completely start before moving on to the next storage node.

For example, if you were to try to upgrade the sample cluster we have used so far (with one management node, two storage nodes, and a SQL node on three physical servers), the process would be as follows:

1. Stop the management node by issuing <id> STOP in the management client, where <id> is the ID of the management node (ID 1 in the sample output from the SHOW command within the management client example earlier in this chapter).

2. Exit the management client.

3. Upgrade the MySQL-ndb-management package or copy the new ndb_mgmd and ndb_mgm binaries to overwrite the old ones in your binary directory.

4. Start the new ndb_mgmd binary from /var/lib/mysql-cluster.

5. Enter the management console, where you should see something like this:

```
ndb_mgm> SHOW
Cluster Configuration
---------------------
[ndbd(NDB)]     2 node(s)
id=2    @10.0.0.2  (Version: 5.0.10, Nodegroup: 0, Master)
id=3    @10.0.0.3  (Version: 5.0.10, Nodegroup: 0)

[ndb_mgmd(MGM)] 1 node(s)
id=1    @10.0.0.1  (Version: 5.0.11)

[mysqld(API)]   3 node(s)
id=4    @10.0.0.1  (Version: 5.0.10)
id=5    @10.0.0.2  (Version: 5.0.10)
id=6    @10.0.0.3  (Version: 5.0.10)
```

Notice how the MGM node is now version 5.0.11, while all other nodes remain 5.0.10.

6. Start upgrading storage nodes. Repeat the following process for each storage node in turn:

- Stop the first storage node by issuing <id> STOP in the management console.

- Upgrade the MySQL-ndb-storage, MySQL-ndb-tools, and MySQL-ndb-extra RPM packages or overwrite all the old ndb* binaries with the new ones.

- Start ndbd again, by using the ndbd -initial command.

- Return to the management console and wait for the status of the node to change from this:

```
id=x    @10.0.0.x  (Version: 5.0.11, starting, Nodegroup: 0)
```

to this:

```
id=x    @10.0.0.x  (Version: 5.0.11, Nodegroup: 0)
```

Move on to the next storage node in the cluster.

When you have completed this process for all storage nodes, you have successfully upgraded your cluster. There is no need to do anything to the SQL nodes that are connected to your cluster, although normally you would want to upgrade them. (The upgrade process is not any different as a result of the cluster subject to the one gotcha covered earlier in this chapter: If you completely remove all the RPMs before reinstalling them, you should comment out the cluster lines in my.cnf, or the installation of the new RPMs will fail.)

Upgrading Through Major Versions

The procedure for upgrading across major versions—for example, from 4.1 to 5.0 or 5.0 to 5.1—is simple but requires a short period of downtime:

1. Enter single-user mode to prevent any changes from being made to your database while you are restoring your backup (see Chapter 3, "Backup and Recovery").

2. Make a backup of your cluster (see Chapter 3).

3. Do a full SQL dump of all databases. (There are bugs in some older versions of MySQL that prevent later versions from reading backup files produced by these versions. You don't want to find that this affects you after you have shut down your cluster and upgraded all the binaries.)

4. Back up `config.ini` (in case you have to change it, for whatever reason, and forget what the original is during the upgrade process).

5. Shut down your cluster (that is, all storage and management nodes).

6. Copy `DataDir` on all storage nodes to a backup folder (this aids quick rollback if you need to go back to the previous version quickly), such as to `/var/lib/mysql-cluster2`.

7. Copy all binaries that start with `ndb` in your MySQL `bin` directory to a backup folder.

8. Upgrade all the MySQL packages on all nodes to the latest versions.

9. Start the management daemon.

10. Start the storage nodes by using `--initial`.

11. Attempt to restore the cluster backup (see Chapter 3).

12. If step 11 fails, drop all tables and databases and restore from your SQL dump.

13. Exit single-user mode.

We suggest that whenever possible, you set up a test cluster on the new version to make sure your data can work nicely. There is a possibility that things might change between major versions, and this might mean, for example, that you would need to increase some parameters in `config.ini` to get things to work. You probably don't want to find this out for the first time when you have to revert to the older version after attempting to upgrade or have to start searching mailing lists for the solution to your problem with your database down.

Other Methods of Starting a Cluster

You might find that it is extremely inconvenient to have to log in to each machine to start `ndbd`, particularly if you have a very large number of nodes in your cluster and/or exotic authentication methods on the servers that make up your cluster which make logging in to lots of servers a time-consuming and tedious process. Several tricks are worth mentioning; the first is to use SSH to start all your data nodes (using the `ssh -t` command to issue a command and then log straight out). You issue the following commands on the management server to completely start your sample cluster (which you should make sure is shut down first):

```
[root@s1 mysql-cluster]# ndb_mgmd
[root@s1 mysql-cluster]# ssh -t 10.0.0.2 ndbd
root@10.0.0.2's password:
Connection to 10.0.0.2 closed.
[root@s1 mysql-cluster]# ssh -t 10.0.3 ndbd
root@10.0.0.3's password:
Connection to 10.0.0.3 closed.
[root@s1 mysql-cluster]# ndb_mgm
-- NDB Cluster -- Management Client --
ndb_mgm> SHOW
Connected to Management Server at: 10.0.0.1:1186
Cluster Configuration
---------------------
[ndbd(NDB)]     2 node(s)
id=2    @10.0.0.2  (Version: 5.0.11, starting, Nodegroup: 0, Master)
id=3    @10.0.0.3  (Version: 5.0.11, starting, Nodegroup: 0, Master)

[ndb_mgmd(MGM)] 1 node(s)
id=1    @10.0.0.1  (Version: 5.0.11)

[mysqld(API)]   3 node(s)
id=4 (not connected, accepting connect from any host)
id=5 (not connected, accepting connect from any host)
id=6 (not connected, accepting connect from any host)
```

Then, after a few minutes, your cluster should start as usual:

```
ndb_mgm> SHOW
Connected to Management Server at: 10.0.0.1:1186
Cluster Configuration
---------------------
[ndbd(NDB)]     2 node(s)
id=2    @10.0.0.2  (Version: 5.0.11, Nodegroup: 0)
id=3    @10.0.0.3  (Version: 5.0.11, Nodegroup: 0, Master)

[ndb_mgmd(MGM)] 1 node(s)
id=1    @10.0.0.1  (Version: 5.0.11)

[mysqld(API)]   3 node(s)
id=4 (Version: 5.0.11)
id=5 (Version: 5.0.11)
id=6 (Version: 5.0.11)
```

If you set up SSH authentication using private/public keys, you can complete this process without using passwords, which means you can script it very easily.

Another trick you can use is to start the ndbd daemon on a node but not actually get it to join the cluster; in this case, it just connects and waits for the management server to instruct it to start. You do this by passing the -n command as an argument to ndbd when you start it (that is, -n = nostart). If you were to start both storage nodes in the sample cluster by using -n, you would get this:

```
ndb_mgm> SHOW
Cluster Configuration
---------------------
[ndbd(NDB)]     2 node(s)
id=2    @10.0.0.2  (Version: 5.0.11, not started)
id=3    @10.0.0.3  (Version: 5.0.11, not started)

[ndb_mgmd(MGM)] 1 node(s)
id=1    @10.0.0.1  (Version: 5.0.11)

[mysqld(API)]   3 node(s)
id=4 (not connected, accepting connect from any host)
id=5 (not connected, accepting connect from any host)
id=6 (not connected, accepting connect from any host)
```

You can start these storage nodes by issuing the *<id>* START command in the management client:

```
ndb_mgm> 2 START
Database node 2 is being started.

ndb_mgm> 3 START
Database node 3 is being started.
```

You can extend this trick further by writing a simple shell script to detect whether ndbd is not running on a node and then get it to "half start" like this so that you can always restart nodes that die from within the management client. This can make dealing with a large cluster much easier because it means you do not have to log in to each server to start the cluster, and as soon as nodes crash or reboot, they will automatically half start, allowing you to completely start them from the management client—eliminating the need for you to actually log in to your storage nodes. A very simple script such as this should do the trick:

```
#!/bin/bash
#
# ndbd_keepalive.sh
#
# Checks that ndbd, the storage daemon for MySQL Cluster,
# is running. If it is not, start it with -n (nostart)
# to allow administrator to start it from within the
# management client
#
```

```
# Usage: /path/to/ndbd_keepalive.sh
#
# This script can be run from crontab every few minutes
#
# (C) Alex Davies 2005.
# You are free to do whatever you like with this script

ps -efl | grep ndbd | grep -v grep  &> /dev/null
if [ "$?"  != 0 ]
then
#       NDBD is dead
#       So, restart it
#       And, log it
        ndbd
        wall "ndbd_keepalive.sh restarted ndbd"
        echo  -n "ndbd_keepalive.sh restarted ndbd: " >> /root/ndbd-restart-log
        date >> /root/ndbd-restart-log
fi
```

Note that you should make sure that the ndbd line contains the full path to the ndbd binary (that is, /usr/local/mysql/bin/ndbd or /usr/sbin/ndbd) if the script does not work without it (which it might not do, particularly if you run it from cron).

You should test the script by starting up your cluster. After the cluster is started, you add the crontab line (crontab -e on most Linux distributions) to the storage nodes, like this:

```
*/2 * * * * /root/ndbd_keepalive.sh
```

This runs the script every 2 minutes.

When the cluster is up and running, you should stop a storage node, and within 3 minutes, it should reconnect so you can start it properly from within the management client:

```
ndb_mgm> SHOW
Connected to Management Server at: 10.0.0.1:1186
Cluster Configuration
---------------------
[ndbd(NDB)]     2 node(s)
id=2     @10.0.0.2  (Version: 5.0.11, Nodegroup: 0)
id=3     @10.0.0.3  (Version: 5.0.11, Nodegroup: 0, Master)

[ndb_mgmd(MGM)] 1 node(s)
id=1     @10.0.0.1  (Version: 5.0.11)

[mysqld(API)]   3 node(s)
id=4     @10.0.0.1  (Version: 5.0.11)
id=5     @10.0.0.2  (Version: 5.0.11)
id=6     @10.0.0.3  (Version: 5.0.11)
```

```
ndb_mgm> 2 STOP
Node 2 has shutdown.
```

At this stage, you should wait 3 minutes for the script to kick in on Storage Node 2 and then restart it. Then, you issue a SHOW command, like this:

```
ndb_mgm> SHOW
Connected to Management Server at: 10.0.0.1:1186
Cluster Configuration
---------------------
[ndbd(NDB)]     2 node(s)
id=2    @10.0.0.2  (Version: 5.0.11, not started)
id=3    @10.0.0.3  (Version: 5.0.11, Nodegroup: 0, Master)

[ndb_mgmd(MGM)] 1 node(s)
id=1    @10.0.0.1  (Version: 5.0.11)

[mysqld(API)]   3 node(s)
id=4    @10.0.0.1  (Version: 5.0.11)
id=5    @10.0.0.2  (Version: 5.0.11)
id=6    @10.0.0.3  (Version: 5.0.11)
```

Notice how Storage Node 2 has now gone to the status "not started." You can now start it by using 2 START:

```
ndb_mgm> 2 START
Database node 2 is being started.
```

If the script restarts a node, it will add a log entry with the date and time in /root/ndbd-restart-log. You could also have it email an administrator so that that person knows to come investigate the cause of the cluster crash and complete the startup process.

You might wonder why the preceding script uses ndbd -n rather than just ndbd (which would start the node completely and not require an <id> START command to be entered into the management client by an administrator). The answer is that you should *never* have a script automatically restart cluster nodes. If cluster nodes die, you should always investigate what the problem is. Of course, it would be perfectly possible to remove the nostart flag from the script and to also write a similar version for ndb_mgmd on the management node; this would allow you to reboot all your machines, and they would then restart the cluster when they started back up. We strongly recommend that you not do this; there are many situations in which you may not actually want both nodes to attempt to start (for example, if you suspect that one node has gotten a corrupt copy of the database, you might want to start the other node(s) in the same node group and then start the dodgy node by using --initial). We believe it is important for an administrator to be around to investigate the cause of node failure.

> **Note**
>
> If you use a script like this, and if you change `config.ini`, you *must* manually stop each storage node and restart it by using `--initial`. If you just stop it and leave it to the script to restart it, the script will simply try to start it every 3 minutes but continue to fail, resulting in downtime for you.

Obtaining, Installing, and Configuring MySQL Cluster on Other Platforms

There is one overriding thought that should be in your mind if you are reading this section: MySQL Cluster is not supported in any way on anything other than the following operating systems:

- Linux (Red Hat, Novell/SUSE)
- Sun Solaris
- IBM AIX
- HP-UX
- Mac OS X

Future versions of MySQL Cluster may add more officially supported platforms as more people use MySQL Cluster in production.

Notice that Windows is *not* included in the list. You should not even consider running it in a production environment on anything other than one of the listed operating systems. The only reason to install it on any other platform should be academic interest and to have a version to play with on whatever machine you use as your desktop.

If you are looking to run a version of MySQL Cluster on your Windows desktop, do yourself a favor and install an emulator such as VirtualPC or VMWare, both of which do a very good job of running any Linux distribution you choose. (CentOS is a good bet if you are fairly new to Linux.) If you have enough RAM, you can run many different virtual machines at the same time and try out things without having to have access to an actual cluster. There has been some work done running MySQL Cluster on Windows, but it is very buggy and incomplete, and we can't understand why you would want to use it.

We should also point out that in a production environment we recommend that you use Linux. This is not because Linux is superior to other operating systems on which MySQL Cluster is supported but simply that the vast majority of users use Linux, and it is the operating system on which MySQL Cluster is best tested and best supported. Solaris is the next most used platform, and in many ways it is similar to Linux. Other platforms are used by a fairly small number of users at the moment, so documentation and the user support available for them is not as good.

If you want to mix platforms, you should be fine, as long as all platforms within the cluster have the same endianness. There are four types, and you should keep to architectures in the same type:

- **Pure big-endian**—Sun SPARC, Motorola 68000, PowerPC 970, IBM System/360
- **Bi-endian, running in big-endian mode by default**—MIPS running IRIX, PA-RISC, most POWER and PowerPC systems
- **Bi-endian, running in little-endian mode by default**—MIPS running Ultrix, most DEC Alpha, IA-64 running Linux
- **Pure little-endian**—Intel x86, AMD64

You can mix the two most common architectures (Intel x86 and AMD64) with no problems, but you cannot mix a Sun SPARC system with an Intel x86 system.

You can install MySQL on Solaris and Mac OS X by downloading the `pkg` format binaries from the MySQL website. You can find more detailed installation instructions in the MySQL manual.

There are also binaries available for HP-UX and IBM AIX. To install on these platforms, you need the `MySQL-max` packages as well as the standard packages.

RAM Usage

MySQL Cluster is an in-memory database in version 5.0, and at the time of this writing, disk-based tables in version 5.1 are in the fairly early stages of testing and are unlikely to be in a generally available version, and therefore available for production use, for quite some time. This means that RAM usage is an important consideration when you are deciding whether MySQL Cluster is the software package for you. If you have an 80GB database, unless you have an extremely large budget, you are not going to be able to use a cluster in MySQL Cluster.

There are several important things to bear in mind about MySQL Cluster. The first is a general rule that your table will occupy significantly more space in NDB than in MyISAM, for the following reasons:

- NDB is fixed width in versions 4.1 and 5.0, so if you have variable-width fields, such as VARCHARs, you will find that the size of the table increases dramatically. Version 5.1 will have true VARCHARs, however.
- NDB stores more indexes than MyISAM. To start with, there is always a primary key in an NDB table; if you don't define one, NDB will create one for you (and hide it from view).

Memory Usage

If you are considering deploying a cluster in MySQL Cluster, in order to determine how many nodes you need and how much RAM you will need installed in each, you need to be able to calculate the memory usage per table.

The first step is calculating the amount of RAM that each row uses in each table. You then multiply the size of each row by the number of rows to get the size of each table. Then you add all the tables together to get the size of the database. Finally, you work out the exact memory usage on each storage node. To finish off, you can test your prediction and see how much RAM the cluster in MySQL Cluster is actually using.

If you have never actually thought about how much space each table occupies, as many administrators do not, this process can be quite daunting. Something that confuses many new administrators and that you should always bear in mind is the difference between bits and bytes: There are 8 bits in 1 byte. In almost all cases, you will be dealing with bytes.

Calculating the RAM Usage of a Table

It is important to remember that MySQL Cluster does not support variable-width fields, which means all rows occupy the same space. This means that VARCHAR fields are actually stored as CHAR fields internally (note that this should change in version 5.1). Many poorly designed tables have massive VARCHAR fields (for example, VARCHAR(200) for email addresses). This is because when using storage engines that support variable-width columns, such as MyISAM, it is easier to make the field far too large than to risk making it too small. However, in MySQL Cluster, such tables take up a colossal quantity of RAM. It is always worth attempting to reduce the size of variable-width fields if at all possible.

The calculation of the memory requirement for NDB tables follows the same principles as for the other table engines, with some differences. We now list the memory requirements for different types of fields.

In the following tables, M refers to the defined size of the string field (for example, in a VARCHAR(200) field, M = 200.) Note that character sets are 1 to 3 bytes in size. If you are unsure of how big your character set is, you can find the information by using the SQL command SHOW CHARACTER SET and viewing the Maxlen field.

TABLE 1.2   **String Types**

String Type	Size
VARCHAR(M)	M × character set size + 2 bytes, rounded up to next multiple of 4
CHAR(M)	M × character set size bytes, rounded up to next multiple of 4
BINARY(M) plus derivatives	Same as CHAR or VARCHAR for VARBINARY
ENUM('value1','value2',...)	1 or 2 bytes, depending on the number of options

String Type	Size
SET('value1','value2',...)	1 to 8 bytes, depending on the number of set members
BLOB, TEXT plus derivatives	If M < 256, then M; otherwise, (M - 256) bytes, rounded up to the next multiple of 2,000 plus 256 bytes

TABLE 1.3 Numeric Types

Integer Type	Size (Round Up to Even 4 Bytes)
TINYINT	1 byte
SMALLINT	2 bytes
MEDIUMINT	3 bytes
INT, INTEGER	4 bytes
BIGINT	8 bytes
FLOAT(p)	4 bytes if $0 <= p <= 24$; 8 bytes if $25 <= p <= 53$
FLOAT	4 bytes
DOUBLE [PRECISION], item REAL	8 bytes
BIT(M)	Approximately $(M+7)/8$ bytes
DECIMAL (A, B)	Complex; see http://dev.mysql.com/doc/refman/5.0/en/storage-requirements.html

TABLE 1.4 Date Types

Data Type	Size (Round Up to Even 4 Bytes)
DATE	3 bytes
DATETIME	8 bytes
TIMESTAMP	4 bytes
TIME	3 bytes
YEAR	1 byte

To calculate DataMemory, you first need to work out how many bytes the fields are going to use. Then you add a fixed row overhead, which is 16 bytes, or 12 bytes if you declare all your columns as NOT NULL. Then, for each ordered index, 10 bytes of storage are used. You get an ordered index for each INDEX you define. In addition, you automatically get one ordered index for each primary key and each unique key you specify, unless you tell it not to create one in the CREATE TABLE syntax. Remember that you can change tables at a later time by using ALTER TABLE or CREATE/DROP INDEX commands within MySQL; this, of course, will change your memory allocation.

However, this is not the complete story if you are trying to work out how much RAM you are going to use; you must take into account the storage space used by primary keys. Each primary key (if you have defined it) or hash index (which NDB automatically creates if you have not defined a primary key) occupies 25 bytes of storage (25 bytes + the size of the key in MySQL 4.1). You add this number to the number you calculated earlier and write this number down as the size of each row.

In addition, for each unique constraint in your schema, other than primary keys, an additional hidden table is created to enforce the constraint. In this hidden table, there are at least two columns. The first columns are the ones that you declared as unique. These columns are treated as the primary key in the hidden table. The other columns in this table make up the primary key from the base table. This hidden table has all the normal space requirements as a regular table (that is, 12 bytes overhead per row). You can see that this causes unique constraints to be quite a bit of extra size overhead. However, this setup does allow for additional speed in accessing constraints, which is discussed further in Chapter 5, "Performance."

You then have to consider the way that NDB stores information: in pages. All data is stored in pages (a page is a certain part of RAM), and each page holds 32,768 bytes of data. Each page of data can store data from only one table (or hidden table). You therefore have to work out how many rows you get per page, which tells you how many pages you need. You divide 32,768 by the number you produced earlier and round the number down. This tells you how many rows you will get per page of 128 bytes.

You next divide the number of rows by the number of rows per page to get the number of pages you need. This is important because you will need to add a fixed overhead per page.

You can now calculate the total memory requirement, in bytes, for one copy (replica) of your table:

(Size of each row × Number of Rows) + (Number of pages × 128)

You repeat this calculation for all tables in your cluster to get a figure for the total memory requirement for one copy of your tables.

Of course, you also want to know how much RAM you need on each storage node. You use the following calculation for this:

(Total memory requirement for one copy of your tables × Number of replicas[3]) / Number of storage nodes

You divide this figure by 1,024 to get kilobytes and finally by another 1,024 to get megabytes.

Remember that this calculation gives you an estimate for the RAM required for data storage. More RAM is required for buffers, temporary storage, and so on; exactly how much depends entirely on the environment, so you need to experiment.

---

3. You will come across this parameter in detail in Chapter 2. It determines how many copies of each piece of data the cluster holds. 2 is a typical value.

A Sample Calculation of the RAM Required for a Table

Because calculating the RAM usage of a table is so complex, this section gives a sample calculation for the following table, which contains both integer and string types, as well as variable- and fixed-width fields:

```
mysql> desc testtable;
+-------+--------------+------+-----+---------+-------+
| Field | Type         | Null | Key | Default | Extra |
+-------+--------------+------+-----+---------+-------+
| id    | int(11)      |      | PRI | 0       |       |
| name  | varchar(60)  |      |     |         |       |
| email | varchar(80)  |      |     |         |       |
| sex   | enum('M','F')|      |     | M       |       |
+-------+--------------+------+-----+---------+-------+
4 rows in set (0.00 sec)
```

This example assumes that the table uses latin1 (so the size of the character set is 1 byte). It also assumes that this table has 500 rows.

The first step is to calculate the size of each row:

- Each INT field occupies 4 bytes.
- Each VARCHAR(60) field occupies 64 bytes (60 + 2, rounded to next multiple of 4).
- Each VARCHAR(80) field occupies 84 bytes (80 + 2, rounded to next multiple of 4).
- Each small ENUM field is 1 byte, rounded to next multiple of 4.
- There are two indexes, so there is a 20-byte overhead per row.

This makes the total size of each row 176 bytes.

You can now divide 32,768 (the maximum size of a page) by 176 to get 186.2, so you know that each page will hold 186 rows. You can therefore work out that for 500 rows, you will need 3 pages. You can now work out the extra overhead of 128 bytes per page: 384 bytes.

Therefore, the RAM required for data storage will be (176 × 500) [Size of row × Number of rows] + (16 × 500) [Number of rows × Fixed overhead per row of 16 bytes] + 384 [Page overhead]. This comes out to 96,000 bytes, or 94KB.

You now have to work out the RAM requirement for indexes, which is easy: 25 bytes per row, so in this case, 12,500 bytes, or 12.2KB.

This gives you the quantity, in data and index RAM requirement, of this one very small, very simple, table. Of course, you need to take account of your total number of nodes and number of replicas; if you have four nodes and two replicas, you divide these figures in half to work out the storage requirement per node (because each node has half of each table).

Of course, there are significant overheads, and it is always a good idea to allow at least an extra 10% for temporary storage and so on—and for a small table, you should add a lot more.

Automatic Methods of Calculating RAM Requirements

At the time of this writing, MySQL has just released a script written by Steward Smith, `ndb_size`, that aims to calculate memory usage for a table automatically. We anticipate that by the time this book is published, this script will be included with MySQL. However, if it is not, you will be able to download if from this book's website, www.mysql-cluster.com.

The idea is that you run the `ndb_size` script on a table before you convert it to NDB so that you can tell if you have enough RAM and get a good idea about what values to set for several configuration options.

To use this script, you need to download the script `ndb_size.pl` as well as the HTML template `ndb_size.tmpl`. You need the following Perl modules installed: `DBD::mysql` and `HTML::Template`. After you download the script, you should execute it with the following parameters:

```
[root@host] perl ndb_size.pl db-name host user password
```

It will create an HTML file that you can view in any web browser.

For example, to calculate the size of the test database on the `localhost` where the password for the `root` account is `mypass`, you would use this command:

```
[root@host] perl ndb_size.pl test localhost root mypass > /path/to/file.htm
```

We do not repeat the output here, but the output is split into sections, all of which are useful. The first section, "Parameter Settings," gives estimates of what you should set the parameters in `config.ini` to. These will tend to be low but give a pretty good estimation. If you want to calculate your RAM usage, you add up the first two lines in the table (`DataMemory (kb)` and `IndexMemory (kn)`) and ignore the rest.

The rest of the report gives a breakdown of memory usage by attributes (tables, indexes, and so on) and then a further breakdown by table.

It is worth noting that the MySQL Cluster version 5.1 figures may change by the time that version is released.

Using MySQL Cluster on 64-Bit Operating Systems

So far we have concentrated on standard systems. Over the past 18 months, the hype surrounding 64-bit processors has increased massively, and many new servers are now able to run in either 64-bit or 32-bit modes.

From the point of view of MySQL Cluster, 64-bit processors have a massive advantage: They can address more RAM. If you have a 32-bit system, you have two problems: First, there is no possibility of the system addressing (that is, using) more than about 4GB of RAM, and second, the system will generally fail to start if the operating system attempts to allocate more than a few gigabytes of RAM in one chunk (for example, to a storage node), with an error such as this:

```
Message: Memory allocation failure
Fault ID: 2327
Problem data: DBTUP could not allocate memory for Page
```

The obvious solution to this is to upgrade to 64-bit hardware and a 64-bit operating system. However, if you want to address the full 4GB of RAM and keep your 32-bit hardware, you can simply run multiple NDBD nodes on the same machines, with `DataMemory` plus `IndexMemory` for each `ndbd` process set to the maximum that you can safely address (say, 2GB). If you do this, you must specify which node group each storage node is a members of, as explained earlier in this chapter, in the section "An Example of a `config.ini` File." You must ensure that you do not have all the nodes in any node group running on the same physical machine; otherwise, failure of that machine will take the whole cluster down.

Calculating the `DataMemory` and `IndexMemory` Parameters

You will see in Chapter 2 that there are actually two separately configurable options that control RAM usage: `DataMemory` and `IndexMemory`. `DataMemory` controls everything except the primary key or hash index that every single row has. (If you do not create a primary key, NDB will create a hash index for you and hide it.) So `DataMemory` includes other regular indexes. `IndexMemory` can be calculated as 25 bytes per row for the primary key and 25 additional bytes for each unique key (due to the hidden table). Additional hidden tables created by secondary hash indexes use `DataMemory`, not `IndexMemory`.

Reducing Memory Usage

If you discover that your current table structure is too large to fit viably into RAM, you have several options. The first, and often most viable, is to normalize the data to eliminate duplicate data. For example, say you have a table like this:

```
PEOPLE
ID                      INT(2)
Name                    VARCHAR (200)
Favorite_color          VARCHAR (100)
```

You might find that you have perhaps five colors, which make up 95% of the colors that people select. If you have, say 1,000,000 rows, you could save yourself a vast amount of RAM by changing the structure to two tables:

```
PEOPLE
ID                      INT(2)
Name                    VARCHAR (200)
COLOR_ID                TINYINT (1)

COLORS
COLOR_ID                TINYINT(1)
Favorite_color          VARCHAR (100)
```

You can then make queries with a simple join.

The second commonly used trick is to reduce the size of variable-width fields that are often set too large. For example, tables often have a very large number of VARCHAR(225) fields defined because whoever produced the table wanted to err on the side of caution, and it worked at the time. However, often the largest field is actually much smaller than that—perhaps 50 bytes. In table engines that support variable-width fields, this is not a problem, but as we have seen, NDB not only does not support variable-width fields (so each VARCHAR(225) field is stored as a CHAR(225) with an additional overhead) but it also stores at least two copies of each piece of data.

To illustrate this point, if we have VARCHAR(225) fields that have 100,000 rows with an average field length of 50 bytes, the following gives an idea of the size the field will use:

- **MyISAM**—0.6MB
- **NDB**—2.7MB × NumberOfReplicas (+ Overheads)

This represents a 350% increase from MyISAM to NDB before you account for the fact that NDB requires at least two copies of each piece of data. If you started off with a very large MyISAM table with lots of these VARCHAR fields, you could require such a ridiculous amount of RAM that the cluster in MySQL Cluster would cease to be a viable and cost-effective solution.

The best solution to this problem is to go back through the applications that use the database and establish what the actual maximum acceptable size is (if they have any validation before inserts or updates) and either reduce it to something sensible or add validation at a sensible level. You can then change the table structure to this new lower size, which makes an enormous difference.

Adding Tables

Now that you have your cluster up and running and understand the principles behind memory usage, you can start to import your existing tables into the cluster.

There are two methods for doing this: You can use a SQL CREATE TABLE statement with ENGINE=NDBCLUSTER or you can use a SQL ALTER TABLE statement, also with ENGINE=NDBCLUSTER.

Using ALTER TABLE

The easiest way to move your table across is simply to alter an existing table. The syntax for this is very simple, and you can carry out this process from any SQL node. You can use the command SHOW TABLE STATUS to check what engine a table has:

```
mysql> SHOW TABLE STATUS FROM dbname LIKE 'tablename';
+-------+------------+---------+------------+------+
| Name  | Engine     | Version | Row_format | Rows |
+-------+------------+---------+------------+------+
| ctest | MyISAM     |      10 | Fixed      |    0 |
+-------+------------+---------+------------+------+
1 row in set (0.01 sec)
```

You also get a lot more statistics, but the interesting one is `Engine`. To change from any other engine to `NDBCLUSTER`, you issue the following commands:

```
mysql> USE test;
mysql> ALTER TABLE tablename ENGINE=NDBCLUSTER;
Query OK, 0 rows affected (3.54 sec)
Records: 0  Duplicates: 0  Warnings: 0
```

This does not tell you very much, so it is worth checking that it has worked:

```
mysql> SHOW TABLE STATUS FROM dbname LIKE 'tablename';
+-------+------------+---------+------------+------+
| Name  | Engine     | Version | Row_format | Rows |
+-------+------------+---------+------------+------+
| ctest | ndbcluster |      10 | Fixed      |    0 |
+-------+------------+---------+------------+------+
1 row in set (0.01 sec)
```

Notice how the engine has changed from `MyISAM` to `ndbcluster`. This means that it has worked.

If you want to be 100% sure that this has worked, you should move over to a SQL node on a different physical machine and see if the table has appeared on it. (Remember that you must create the database that the table is in first of all on all SQL nodes.) If it has appeared, you know for certain that your cluster is working and that this table is clustered.

Using CREATE TABLE

You used the second method, the `CREATE TABLE` command, when you created the `ctest` table during the MySQL Cluster installation process. To convert a database to `NDBCLUSTER`, you get a SQL statement of the table structure, as in this example:

```
CREATE TABLE `test`.`ctest` (
`field1` int( 11 ) NOT NULL default '0',
`field2` char( 11 ) NOT NULL default '0',
`whattodo` enum( 'Y', 'N' ) NOT NULL default 'Y'
) ENGINE = MYISAM DEFAULT CHARSET = latin1;
```

Now, you simply replace the last line with this:

```
) ENGINE = NDBCLUSTER DEFAULT CHARSET = latin1;
```

Then you execute the query at a SQL node. You should get an empty table created in the new format . If you are trying to move a table into NDB, we recommend the following course of action:

1. For each table in the original database, dump the structure so you have a SQL query that will create the table.

2. Change ENGINE = *whatever* to ENGINE = NDBCLUSTER for all tables within the SQL file.

3. Move the database to dbname-old and create a new database dbname on all SQL nodes.

4. Import your newly modified SQL code so you create the same (empty) tables within the database with ENGINE=NDBCLUSTER.

5. Move the data across by running the following query for each table:

```
INSERT INTO `dbname`.`tablename` SELECT * FROM `dbname-old`.`tablename` ;
```

This copies all your data from the old table to the new table.

Common Errors While Importing Tables

You are most likely to experience an error when importing data into a table. The following sections cover some of the common errors you may experience while carrying out the procedures covered earlier in this chapter.

ERROR 1114 (HY000) at line 227: The table 'table_log' is full

This error means that you do not have enough DataMemory or IndexMemory. You will learn how to change these values in Chapter 2, but for now you just need to know how to find out what values you should set them to. In theory, you should either work it out manually or use a script such as ndb_size.pl, as discussed earlier in this chapter. However, if you want to find out your actual usage, you can use the command ALL DUMP 1000. In the management client, you issue ALL DUMP 1000 like this:

```
ndb_mgm> ALL DUMP 1000
Sending dump signal with data:
0x000003e8 Sending dump signal with data:
0x000003e8
```

You should now see the recorded memory usage of each node in the cluster log on the management daemon. You exit the management client and tail this log file:

```
ndb_mgm> exit
[root@s1 mysql-cluster]# ls
config.ini  config.ini.threenode ndb_1_cluster.log  ndb_1_out.log  ndb_1.pid
[root@s1 mysql-cluster]# tail -4 ndb_1_cluster.log
date time [MgmSrvr] INFO  -- Node 3: Data usage is 0%(19 32K pages of total 2560)
date time [MgmSrvr] INFO  -- Node 3: Index usage is 1%(34 8K pages of total 2336)
date time [MgmSrvr] INFO  -- Node 2: Data usage is 0%(19 32K pages of total 2560)
date time [MgmSrvr] INFO -- Node 2: Index usage is 1%(34 8K pages of total 2336)
```

> **Note**
> The number after the `tail` command should be double the number of storage nodes because
> you are telling tail how many lines to display (starting at the bottom of the file), and each stor-
> age node will produce two lines of log after you issue this command.

Now all you need is some simple math to work out how much `DataMemory` and `IndexMemory` are currently being used. To work this out, you choose the highest value for the data usage and index usage if there is a difference between the results for the different storage nodes (which there should not be).

`19 32K pages of total 2560` means that the actual usage is $19 \times 32KB$, which is 2560KB (which is 2.5MB). Similarly, `34 8K pages of total 2336` means 2336KB of space.

You should make sure that your values in `config.ini` are significantly larger than the mini-mum values you have just calculated because there will be times when storage nodes will need more space for temporary tables, and you don't want to run the risk of a table suddenly filling up and hitting its size limit, causing downtime.

ERROR 1005 (HY000) at line x: Can't create table './dbname/tablename.frm' (errno: 4242)

This error means "too many indexes." As you'll learn in Chapter 2, you need to increase `MaxNoOfUniqueIndexes` and/or `MaxNoOfOrderedIndexes`.

ERROR 1005 (HY000) at line x: Can't create table './dbname/tablename.frm' (errno: 4335)

This error indicates a problem with too many auto-increment fields. Only one auto-incre-ment column is allowed per table. Having a table without a primary key uses an auto-incre-mented hidden key. That is, a table without a primary key cannot have an auto-incremented column, and a table with a primary key cannot have two auto-incremented columns.

ERROR 1015 (HY000): Can't lock file (errno: 4006)

This error means "increase `MaxNoOfConcurrentTransactions`." When the MySQL server needs to start a transaction, it looks for a transaction object in a pool. Each object in this pool is connected to a certain data node. When starting a scan of a table, a transaction object is also used. Thus, in the worst case, a connection could potentially allocate the following at the same time on one data node:

```
Max number of tables in query + 1 (transaction) + 1 (short term usage)
```

This means if say you use a maximum of 20 table joins, you would get a maximum of 22 transaction objects per connection, so you can work out what value to set `MaxNoOfConcurrentTransactions` to. Of course, 22 would be a worst-case scenario. Most transactions use 1 or 2 transaction objects, but you should be aware that this is an error that you may encounter.

Chapter 2 provides more information on changing `config.ini` parameters.

ERROR 1050 (42S01): Table 'ctest' already exists

This error may be generated by a query such as this:

```
mysql> create table ctest (i int) engine=ndbcluster;
```

It means the cluster is not working. As a preventive measure, if the cluster is not working, you will not be able to create tables simply because the SQL node does not know what tables actually exist in NDB format and so would run the risk of overwriting the tables that are already stored in the cluster.

In this case, you should go back to ndb_mgm and make sure all nodes are connected; if they are not, you should get them to connect. If all the storage nodes are connected, you should make sure that the /etc/my.cnf configuration on each storage node is correct and points to the correct management daemon.

"Out of operation records in transaction coordinator"

This error can occur during migration of tables, particularly during INSERT INTO...SELECT style queries because each INSERT becomes an operation. The solution is to increase the parameter MaxNoOfConcurrentOperations in config.ini.

2

Configuration

You have already seen how to produce a basic configuration for a cluster. However, you will almost certainly find that you want to specify some, if not all, of the optional configuration settings; this chapter explains what they all do.

All these settings go in the config.ini file, which is often placed in the DataDir of the management node (conventionally /var/lib/mysql-cluster). If you change this file, you will have to completely restart the cluster either following a process very similar to that of an online upgrade (as described in Chapter 1, "Installation") or, by doing a backup, a total cluster shutdown, and a re-import.

> **Note**
> Technically, the config.ini file can go anywhere, as long as you are in that directory when you start the management daemon (ndb_mgmd). However, we strongly suggest that you keep it on your DataDir, where all the other files that the management daemon will create (such as log files) will go.

To do a rolling online configuration change, you follow these steps:

1. Change the configuration file as desired (for example, increase DataMemory).
2. Stop your management daemon by using *<id>* STOP, where *<id>* is the ID of the management node, as displayed in the management client (ndb_mgm).
3. Start your management daemon.
4. Carry out the following process for each storage node (one node at a time):

> **Note**
> You can do more than one storage node at a time. The actual restriction is that you must have one node per node group remaining up at all times, but we don't suggest that you do this because if you change only one node at a time, (a) if it goes wrong, you have only one node down and (b) you know exactly which node is causing problems.

- Stop the storage node by using *<id>* STOP, where *<id>* is the ID of the storage node, as displayed in the management client.

- Start the storage node by using ndbd --initial. The --initial option is required only for certain parameters; however, it is always safe to use (it may just make the restart take slightly more time). This is where the upgrade actually takes place; in other words, when the node starts, it is upgraded.

- Wait for the storage node to fully start before moving on to the next node. To determine that it is done, look at the results of a SHOW command in the management client.

The parameters that require the --initial option for the ndbd restart are ones that change the on-disk format, such as NoOfFragmentLogFiles, but it is always safer to use it. There is no disadvantage except for a small increase in the time the node takes to restart.

To do a backup and restart, you follow these steps:

1. Make a backup of the cluster.
2. Shut down the entire cluster.
3. Restart all the nodes by using the --initial option.
4. Reimport your backup.

Luckily, there aren't very many parameters that require a process this severe. This process is required only when an option change requires the data to be partitioned in a different fashion. The following changes require this:

- Changing NoOfReplicas
- Adding/removing data nodes

This chapter is split into several sections: one that covers configuration options that apply to all nodes, one that covers management nodes, one that covers storage nodes, and one that covers SQL nodes. Each of these sections covers the options that can be used as defaults for all nodes of that type.

It is worth pointing out that the parameter names in MySQL Cluster are no longer case-sensitive. In older versions of 4.1, all the parameters were case-sensitive. So, for example, you can specify Id=3 or ID=3 or id=3, and they will all work the same.

The Structure of config.ini

The config.ini file has several parts. You have already been introduced to a very simple config.ini file. You can find a list of all the sections and what you can put in them in the Chapter 1.

The `config.ini` file has sections for settings for management, storage, and SQL nodes. Within each section are defaults that apply to all nodes of that type, and you must have one section per node (even if you have no parameters in it).

These are the sections:

```
#
# STORAGE NODES
#

[NDBD DEFAULT]
# In here you put the settings that apply to all storage nodes

[NDBD]
# In here you put the settings for one individual storage node
# You must have one [NBDD] section for EACH storage node


#
# MANAGEMENT NODES
#

[NDB_MGMD DEFAULT]
# In here you put the settings that apply to all management nodes

[NDB_MGMD]
# In here you put the settings for one individual management node
# You must have one [NBD_MGM] section for EACH management node


#
# SQL NODES
#

[MYSQLD DEFAULT]
# In here you put the settings that apply to all SQL nodes

[MYSQLD]
# In here you put the settings for one individual SQL node
# You must have one [MYSQLD] section for EACH SQL node
```

Note that this block of text is in code form. We suggest that you use this as your `config.ini` template; you can then easily add parameters to the correct block. You can download this file from this book's website, www.mysql-cluster.com.

The following sections cover the parameters you can set in each section.

All Nodes

Two options can go under the [NDBD], [NDB_MGM], and [MYSQLD] sections: Id and HostName. It is conventional to define HostName for all nodes.

Id

Each node in a cluster has a unique identity, ranging from 1 to 64, inclusive. This ID is used by all internal cluster messages for addressing the node, and it is also used to identify the node in log files and create output files that can be identified with the node. If you do not set this, the management daemon assigns each node the next free ID to each node that connects (and it assigns itself an ID of 1).

If you choose to run multiple management nodes, you *must* set the IDs. If you are running a large cluster, you may want to set the IDs so you know without question that the same node will always have the same ID, however often it is perfectly satisfactory to let the management daemon just assign the IDs.

HostName

The HostName parameter defines the hostname or IP address of the computer that the storage node is to reside on (for example, HostName=10.0.0.2).

We suggest that you use IP addresses whenever possible. If you use hostnames, you need to make sure that both your forward and reverse DNS lookups are in perfect order, and if you experience problems, the first thing you should try is to switch the hostnames for IP addresses and see if that fixes the problem.

Management Nodes

As with all three types of node, there are parameters that you should set for all nodes (and it makes sense to set these in the DEFAULT section rather than in each node's section) and some that you must set individually.

Parameters to Define for All Management Nodes (NDB_MGMD_DEFAULT)

All the following options *can* go under [NDB_MGM] headers in addition to the DEFAULT section. A typical cluster has only one management daemon, but it is possible to define two or more. The procedure for doing so is covered later in this section. Either way, it makes sense to define settings that apply to all management nodes if you have more than one in the DEFAULT section.

PortNumber

The PortNumber parameter specifies the port number on which the management server listens for configuration requests and management commands. The default, which we suggest you not change, is 1186. You can specify different ports for different management nodes, but we recommend that you do not do so. If you wanted to run multiple management nodes on one server (for example, if you had two separate clusters that shared a management server), you could create two config.ini files (in different folders) with different port numbers and data directories and start both daemons, which would not then conflict.

LogDestination

The LogDestination parameter specifies where the management daemon will send the cluster logs it creates. There are three options in this regard: CONSOLE, SYSLOG, and FILE.

CONSOLE outputs the log to stdout (that is, it displays it on the screen of the server, which is great for debugging when you have the screen in front of you but not so great if you have your servers "headless" in a rack elsewhere). This is easy to set:

```
LogDestination=CONSOLE
```

SYSLOG sends the log to a syslog facility; you must provide a facility parameter for this, with possible values being auth, authpriv, cron, daemon, ftp, kern, lpr, mail, news, syslog, user, uucp, local0, local1, local2, local3, local4, local5, local6 and local7 (not every facility is necessarily supported by every operating system). Here's an example:

```
LogDestination=SYSLOG:facility=syslog
```

FILE pipes the cluster log output to a regular file on the same machine. You can also set the following three parameters:

- **filename**—The name of the log file. The default is ndb_*<NODEID>*_cluster.log (where *<NODEID>* is the node ID of the management node, typically 1).
- **maxsize**—The maximum size to which the file can grow before logging rolls over to a new file. When this occurs, the old log file is renamed by appending .*x* to the filename, where *x* is the next number not yet used with this name. The default is 1000000.
- **maxfiles**—The maximum number of log files. The default is 6.

The following is an example of a configuration line:

```
LogDestination=FILE:filename=my-cluster.log,maxsize=500000,maxfiles=4
```

It is also possible to specify multiple log destinations by using a semicolon-delimited string:

```
LogDestination=CONSOLE;SYSLOG:facility=syslog;FILE:filename=/var/log/cluster-log
```

Again, you can specify different logging levels for different management nodes, but we suggest that you do not do so.

DataDir

The DataDir parameter sets the directory where output files from the management server will be placed. These files include process output files and the daemon's process ID file, and they may include cluster log files, depending on the settings of LogDestination.

ArbitrationRank

The ArbitrationRank parameter is used to define which nodes can act as arbitrators. Only management nodes and SQL nodes can be arbitrators. Therefore, this configuration option works identically if it is in an [NDB_MGM] section or a [MYSQLD] section of config.ini (the only difference is the different default values of the two different types of nodes).

ArbitrationRank can take one of the following values:

- **0**—The node will never be used as an arbitrator.
- **1**—The node has high priority; that is, it will be preferred as an arbitrator over low-priority nodes.
- **2**—The node has a low priority; that is, it will not be used as an arbitrator unless there are no nodes with higher priority available.

Normally, you should configure all management servers as high-priority arbitrators by setting their ArbitrationRank parameter to 1 (the default value) and setting this parameter for all SQL nodes to 2 (also the default).

Parameters to Define for Each Management Node (NDB_MGMD)

You should specify a Hostname parameter and, if you are setting Id values for other nodes in the cluster for the sake of neatness or if you are using multiple management nodes, you should set Id as well. Other than that, there is no need to set any other parameters, as long as the compulsory ones are fixed in the DEFAULT section.

An Example of a Management Section of a config.ini File

The following is an example of a configuration with one management node:

```
[NDB_MGMD DEFAULT]
# Listen on default port, 1186
PortNumber=1186
# Log to console, syslog and also to a file
# cluster-log in /var/log/.
LogDestination=CONSOLE;SYSLOG:facility=syslog;FILE:filename=/var/log/cluster-log
# Store files in /var/lib/mysql-cluster
DataDir=/var/lib/mysql-cluster
#All management nodes should be high priority for arbitration.
```

```
ArbitrationRank=1

[NDB_MGMD]
# ID of 1 (standard for management node)
Id = 1
# Enter IP instead of xx.xx.xx.xx
Hostname = xx.xx.xx.xx
```

You can find an example using two management nodes at the end of this chapter, in the section "Using Multiple Management Nodes." Because there is only one management node in the preceding example, you have probably noticed that it would be functionally identical to ignore the DEFAULT section and just use the following:

```
[NDB_MGMD]
Id = 1
Hostname = xx.xx.xx.xx
PortNumber=1186
LogDestination=CONSOLE;SYSLOG:facility=syslog;FILE:filename=/var/log/cluster-log
DataDir=/var/lib/mysql-cluster
ArbitrationRank=1
```

However, it is good practice to use the DEFAULT section, if possible.

Storage Nodes

All the following options go under the [NDBD_DEFAULT] or [NDBD] headings in config.ini.

For each parameter that defines a memory size, it is possible to use k, M, or G as a suffix to indicate units of 1024, 1024^2, or 1024^3.

Parameters to Define for All Storage Nodes (NDBD_DEFAULT)

There are some parameters that you *must* define for all nodes. For example, setting NoOfReplicas to different values for different nodes will not work. Also, it does not make sense to set different values for DataMemory and IndexMemory because if you do, you will find yourself limited to the lowest value (storage nodes must have roughly the same amount of data). It therefore makes sense to put these parameters in the DEFAULT section.

NoOfReplicas

The global parameter NoOfReplicas, which can be set only in the [NDBD DEFAULT] section, defines the number of replicas (copies) of each fragment of data stored in the cluster. This parameter also specifies the size of node groups. (Remember that a *node group* is a set of nodes that all store the same information.)

Node groups are formed implicitly. The first node group is formed by the set of data nodes with the lowest node IDs, the next node group by the set of the next-lowest node identities, and so on.

There is no default value for NoOfReplicas (it must be specified); the maximum possible value is 4. You *can* set it to 1, but of course that gives you no redundancy, so we recommend that you set it to 2 or more.

You should bear in mind that your total number of storage nodes should be a multiple of NoOfReplicas and a power of 2, if possible (clearly, this is not possible if NoOfReplicas is set to 3), so if you have NoOfReplicas set to 2, you should have 2, 4, 8, or 16 (and so on) nodes. This is due to the way that MySQL Cluster currently partitions the data, and this is expected to become less important in version 5.1 due to the fact that you will be able to control the partitioning mechanism in that version.

Changing the setting for NoOfReplicas for an active cluster requires that you take down the entire cluster and re-import the data, so generally you should avoid changing this parameter after you have your cluster set up.

DataDir

The DataDir parameter specifies the directory where local checkpoints, trace files, log files, process ID files, and error logs are placed. This can be specified for each individual storage node, but we recommend that you define it in the DEFAULT section to avoid confusion, and we recommend that you set it to /var/lib/mysql-cluster, which is the conventional location. There is no default value; you must specify this either in the [NDBD_DEFAULT] section or in each separate [NDBD] section.

DataMemory and IndexMemory

DataMemory and IndexMemory are parameters that specify the size of memory segments used to store the actual records and their indexes. Although you do not have to set these, the defaults are very low, and you are unlikely to be able to import anything larger than a token table with them.

When setting these parameters, it may be helpful to look up the syntax of the ALL DUMP 1000 command in Appendix B, "Management Commands," and also the detailed example of its usage in Chapter 2, "Configuration."

We strongly recommended that you set DataMemory and IndexMemory to the same values for all nodes, which is why we also suggest that you define these parameters in the [NDBD_DEFAULT] section. Because data is distributed evenly over all nodes in the cluster, your storage nodes will be able to use only as much as the smallest setting, so there is really no point in setting different values for different nodes.

DataMemory and IndexMemory can be changed, but decreasing either of them can be risky; doing so can easily lead to a node or even an entire cluster being unable to restart due to insufficient memory space. Increasing these values should be fine, but it is important that such upgrades be performed in the same manner as software upgrades, following the procedure outlined at the beginning of this chapter.

DataMemory defines the amount of RAM that is available for the storage node to keep its data in. *Data* in this context means the actual data in the table *and* all indexes apart from the primary (hashed) key.

If you set this parameter too low, you get "table is full" errors when you try to add more data. If you set it too high, the system may start to swap (that is, use the hard drive as RAM) excessively and become unstable. We suggest that when you are importing your initial data, you set this to 70% of your system RAM size. After you have your tables imported, you can use the ALL DUMP 1000 command (see Appendix B and Chapter 1 for more details) to see how much RAM is actually being used, and you can lower this value to be that plus a sensible amount for growth and temporary usage.

You set the DataMemory parameter as a number plus the unit (for example, DataMemory=1024MB). We suggest that you never set this to 100% of your system RAM; if you need that much DataMemory, it is time to add more RAM to your system.

Something that has not been previously discussed that you should be aware of is that DataMemory is also used for UNDO information: For each update, a copy of the unaltered record is allocated in DataMemory. It is therefore necessary to allocate enough memory to handle the largest transactions performed by applications using the cluster. You should avoid large transactions for this and the following reasons:

- Large transactions are not any faster than smaller ones.
- Large transactions increase the number of operations that are lost and must be repeated in the event of transaction failure.
- Large transactions use more memory.

The default value for DataMemory is 80MB, and the minimum value is 1MB. There is no maximum size, but the node should not start swapping when the limit is reached.

IndexMemory defines the amount of RAM that is available for the storage node to keep its hash indexes (that is, primary keys) in. Similar problems occur with IndexMemory as with DataMemory if you set the value too high or low. We suggest that you set IndexMemory to 15% of your system RAM size to start with and adjust it as for DataMemory after your data is imported. It is set identically to DataMemory, with a number followed by units (for example, IndexMemory=128MB).

The default value for IndexMemory is 18MB, and the minimum value is 1MB.

FileSystemPath

The `FileSystemPath` parameter specifies the directory where all files created for metadata, REDO logs, UNDO logs, and data files are placed on the storage node. The default is the directory specified by `DataDir`. Note that this directory must exist before the `ndbd` process is initiated.

The storage daemon creates a subdirectory in the directory specified in `FileSystemPath` for the node's file system. This subdirectory contains the node ID. For example, if the node ID is 2, then this subdirectory is named `ndb_2_fs`. If you leave this at the default and set `DataDir` to `/var/lib/mysql-cluster`, you will get your `FileSystemPath` set to `/var/lib/mysql-cluster/ndb_X_fs/`, where X is the node ID of the storage daemon.

You can set `FileSystemPath` to a different value for each storage node, but we suggest that you not do this. Similarly, we cannot think of many instances in which it would be particularly beneficial to keep the `FileSystemPath` outside the default location (if you have multiple disks it may be a good idea to put this onto a different physical disk to spread out the write operations).

BackupDataDir

It is possible to specify the directory in which backups are placed. By default, this directory is `FileSystemPath/BACKUP`, which in turn defaults to `DataDir/BACKUP` unless you have defined `FileSystemPath`. There should be no reason to change this unless you have multiple hard drives and want to insure against drive failure, in which case you could set `BackupDataDir` to a folder on a separate hard drive.

Transaction Parameters

The next three parameters are important because they affect the number of parallel transactions and the sizes of transactions that can be handled by the system. `MaxNoOfConcurrentTransactions` sets the number of parallel transactions possible in a node and `MaxNoOfConcurrentOperations` (and its partner parameter `MaxNoOfLocalOperations`) sets the number of records that can be in an update phase or locked simultaneously.

These parameters (especially `MaxNoOfConcurrentOperations`) are likely targets for users setting specific values and not using the default value. The default value is set for small clusters using small transactions, in order to ensure that they do not use excessive memory. If you make extensive use of transactions in an application, it is very likely that you will have some large transactions and will therefore have to increase these parameters.

MaxNoOfConcurrentTransactions

Transaction records are allocated to individual MySQL servers, and generally there is at least one transaction record allocated per connection that is using any table in the cluster. For this reason, you should ensure that there are more transaction records in the cluster than there are concurrent connections to all MySQL servers in the cluster (and a lot more if you have individual transactions using multiple tables).

The default setting for the `MaxNoOfConcurrentTransactions` parameter is 4096, which should be sufficient for all but the most heavily laden clusters. This parameter *must* be set to the same value for all cluster nodes.

Changing this parameter is never safe and can cause a cluster to crash. When a node crashes, one of the nodes (the oldest surviving node) builds up the transaction state of all transactions ongoing in the crashed node at the time of the crash. It is thus important that this node have as many transaction records as the failed nodes; in other words, it is a good idea to have this number set significantly higher than you anticipate you will ever use.

MaxNoOfConcurrentOperations and MaxNoOfLocalOperations

When performing transactions of only a few operations each and not involving a great many records, there is no need to set this parameter very high. When performing large transactions involving many records, you should set this parameter higher.

Records are kept for each transaction updating cluster data, both in the transaction coordinator (a randomly chosen storage node) and in the nodes where the actual updates are performed. These records contain state information needed in order to find UNDO records for rollbacks, lock queues, and other purposes.

The `MaxNoOfConcurrentOperations` parameter should therefore be set to the number of records to be updated simultaneously in transactions, divided by the number of cluster data nodes. For example, in a cluster that has 4 data nodes and that is expected to handle 1,000,000 concurrent updates using transactions, you should set this value to 1,000,000 / 4 = 250,000. Of course, you want to build in a safety margin, so you should set the value higher than this.

Read queries that set locks also cause operation records to be created. Some extra operations should be allocated to accommodate cases where the distribution is not perfect over the nodes.

When queries make use of the unique hash index (which most complex queries can be assumed to do at some stage), there are actually two operation records used per record in the transaction: The first record represents the read in the index table (which is a completely separate and hidden table), and the second handles the operation on the base table.

The default value for `MaxNoOfConcurrentOperations` is 32768. If it is exceeded, you get the error message "Out of operation records in transaction coordinator."

`MaxNoOfConcurrentOperations` normally handles a second parameter that can be configured separately. The second parameter, `MaxNoOfLocalOperations`, specifies how many operation records are to be local to the node and is calculated as $1.1 \times$ `MaxNoOfConcurrentOperations` by default (in other words, each node can handle up to 10% more than the average for all nodes).

A very large transaction performed on an eight-node cluster requires as many operation records as there are reads, updates, and deletions involved in the transaction. Therefore, the chances are that you will want to set MaxNoOfLocalOperations higher than the default (that is, 10% greater than MaxNoOfConcurrentOperations) if you are dealing with large transactions. If it is necessary to configure the system for one very large transaction, it is a good idea to configure the two parts separately with MacNoOfLocalOperations set much higher than MaxNoOfConcurrentOperations because this parameter cannot be "spread out" over many nodes.

Transaction Temporary Storage

The next set of parameters is used to define the temporary storage available to the storage nodes when executing a query that is part of a cluster transaction. All records are released when the query is completed and the cluster is waiting for the commit or rollback.

The default values for these parameters are adequate in most situations. However, users who need to support transactions involving large numbers of rows or operations may need to increase these values to enable better parallelism over the cluster. On the other hand, users whose applications require relatively small transactions can decrease the values in order to save memory.

MaxNoOfConcurrentIndexOperations

For queries that use a unique hash index, a temporary set of operation records are used during a query's execution phase. The MaxNoOfConcurrentIndexOperations parameter sets the size of that pool of records available for such use. Thus this record is allocated only while you're executing a part of a query, and as soon as this part has been executed, the record is released. (The states needed to handle the other phases in a transaction's life, aborts and commits, are handled by the normal operation records where the pool size is set by the parameter MaxNoOfConcurrentOperations.)

The default value of MaxNoOfConcurrentIndexOperations is 8192. It should be pointed out that only in rare cases of extremely high parallelism using unique hash indexes should it be necessary to increase this value. Using a smaller value is possible and can save memory if you are certain that a high degree of parallelism is not required for your cluster.

MaxNoOfFiredTriggers

A record is created when an operation is performed that affects a unique hash index. Inserting or deleting a record in a table with unique hash indexes or updating a column that is part of a unique hash index "fires" an insert or a deletion into the index table. The resulting record is used to represent this index table operation while waiting for the original operation that fired it to complete. This operation is short lived but can still require a large number of records in its pool for situations with many parallel write operations on a base table containing a set of unique hash indexes.

The default value of `MaxNoOfFiredTriggers` is 4000, which is sufficient in most situations. In some cases, you can even decrease this value if you feel that the need for parallelism in the cluster is not high.

TransactionBufferMemory

The memory affected by the `TransactionBufferMemory` parameter is used for tracking operations fired when updating index tables and reading unique indexes. This memory is used to store the key and column information for these operations. It is only very rarely that the value for this parameter needs to be altered from the default.

It is possible to change a similar buffer used for read and write operations by changing a compile-time buffer. See "`TransactionBufferMemory`" at the online documentation pages (http://dev.mysql.com/doc/refman/5.0/en/mysql-cluster-db-definition.html) for more details on this parameter, which you are unlikely to need to change.

The default value for `TransactionBufferMemory` is 1MB.

Scans and Buffering

Table and range scans are used during transactions, and there are certain maximum values you need to set. Several buffers are also used. With all these parameters, the defaults will probably work for most clusters, but you may need to increase them. If you are able to reduce them, you will typically save RAM.

MaxNoOfConcurrentScans

The `MaxNoOfConcurrentScans` parameter is used to control the number of parallel table or range scans that can be performed in the cluster. Each transaction coordinator (a randomly picked storage node) can handle the number of parallel scans defined for this parameter.

Each scan query is performed by scanning all partitions in parallel (for performance reasons). Each partition scan uses a "scan record" in the node where the partition is located, the number of "scan records" being the value of this parameter multiplied by the number of nodes.

Scans are typically performed in one of two cases. The first of these cases occurs when no hash or ordered index exists to handle the query, in which case the query is executed by performing a full table scan (which can be very slow). The second case is encountered when there is no hash index to support the query but there is an ordered index. Using the ordered index means executing a parallel range scan. Because the order is kept on the local partitions only, it is necessary to perform the index scan on all partitions, which may involve communicating with other storage nodes that hold other partitions (or fragments) of the data.

The default value of `MaxNoOfConcurrentScans` is 256. The maximum value is 500.

MaxNoOfLocalScans

The `MaxNoOfLocalScans` parameter specifies the number of local scan records that can take place at any one time on each storage node. You might want to increase this value if many of your table scans are not fully parallelized (that is, able to be executed on many nodes at the same time).

The default value for this parameter is the value for `MaxNoOfConcurrentScans` multiplied by the total number of storage nodes in the cluster.

BatchSizePerLocalScan

The `BatchSizePerLocalScan` parameter is used to calculate the number of lock records that needs to exist to handle the concurrent scan operations. If you increase `MaxScanBatchSize` (defined for SQL nodes later in this chapter, in the section "Parameters to Define for All SQL Nodes (`MYSQLD_DEFAULT`)"), you should also increase this parameter. The default is 64.

LongMessageBuffer

The `LongMessageBuffer` parameter defines the size of the internal buffer that is used for passing messages within individual nodes and between nodes. Although it is highly unlikely that this would need to be changed, it is configurable. By default this parameter is set to 1MB.

Logging and Checkpointing

Storage nodes do a large amount of logging to various local log files as part of their operation. This logging is mostly not logging in the traditional sense of error logs and so on but involves logging of recent transactions. These logs are used only in the event of a full cluster shutdown, but they are important because without them, if you suffer a full cluster shutdown, you will not be able to restart your cluster.

NoOfFragmentLogFiles

The `NoOfFragmentLogFiles` parameter sets the number of REDO log files that the storage node will keep. REDO log files are organized in a ring: The cluster creates a new file when the last one gets 16MB and will continue creating until it has created `NoOfFragmentLogFiles` groups of 4 files, at which point it goes back to the beginning and starts overwriting the older files.

It is extremely important that the first and last log files (sometimes referred to as the *head* and *tail* log files, respectively) do not meet; when they approach one another too closely, the node begins aborting all transactions encompassing updates due to not having enough room for new log records.

A REDO log record is not removed until three local checkpoints have been completed since that log record was created. Checkpointing frequency is determined by its own set of configuration parameters, discussed later in this chapter, with the `TimeBetweenLocalCheckpoints` and `TimeBetweenGlobalCheckpoints` parameters. Clearly, if you increase the time between checkpoints such that the head and tail of the `REDO` logs come close to each other, you should increase the value of `NoOfFragmentLogFiles`.

The default `NoOfFragmentLogFiles` parameter value is 8, which means eight sets of four 16MB files, for a total of 512MB. (Note that `REDO` log space must be allocated in blocks of 64MB, or four files of 16MB.) In scenarios that require a great many updates, the value for `NoOfFragmentLogFiles` may need to be set as high as 300 or even higher in order to provide sufficient space for `REDO` logs. If you have this sort of requirement, you are probably going to need a very fast disk drive (for example, RAID or SCSI), so you must make sure that the cluster is not held up writing `REDO` logs to disk.

If the checkpointing is slow and there are so many writes to the database that the log files are full and the log tail cannot be cut without jeopardizing recovery, all updating transactions are aborted with internal error code 410, or "Out of log file space temporarily." This condition prevails until a checkpoint has completed and the log tail can be moved forward.

MaxNoOfSavedMessages

The `MaxNoOfSavedMessages` parameter sets the maximum number of trace files that will be kept before old ones are overwritten. Trace files are generated when, for whatever reason, the node crashes and are very useful for debugging. You need them if you are trying to report a bug to a developer or if someone else on the mailing list asks you for them, as they can help determine what the cluster was doing at the exact moment it crashed.

The default is 25 trace files. We suggest that you do not change this.

Metadata Objects

Metadata objects are pretty much everything within your cluster, including database tables, system tables, indexes, and so on. You will have to increase some of these parameters if you are attempting to import anything larger than a token database because the defaults are often very low. This is especially true for `MaxNoOfAttributes`.

MaxNoOfAttributes

The `MaxNoOfAttributes` parameter sets the number of attributes (including fields, indexes, and primary keys) that can be defined in the cluster.

The default value for this parameter is 1000, with the minimum possible value being 32. There is no maximum. Each attribute consumes around 200 bytes of storage per node (even if it is not used) due to the fact that all metadata is fully replicated on the servers.

This is quite a common limit to hit, and you are likely to be greeted with error 708: "No more attribute metadata records (increase `MaxNoOfAttributes`)" if you try importing a big table without first increasing this parameter.

MaxNoOfTables

The MaxNoOfTables parameter might appear fairly self-explanatory, but remember that a table is allocated for each table, unique hash index, *and* ordered index, even though in the case of indexes, it is hidden from view. This parameter sets the maximum number of table objects for the cluster as a whole.

For each attribute that has a BLOB data type, an extra table is also used to store most of the BLOB data. These tables must also be taken into account when defining the total number of tables.

The default value of this parameter is 128, the minimum is 8, and the maximum is 1600. Each table object consumes approximately 20KB per node, regardless of whether it is used.

MaxNoOfOrderedIndexes

For each ordered index in the cluster, an object is allocated to describe what is being indexed and in which storage segments it resides. Each unique index and primary key has both an ordered index and a hash index.

The default value of the MaxNoOfOrderedIndexes parameter is 128. Each object consumes approximately 10KB of data per node, regardless of whether it is used.

MaxNoOfUniqueHashIndexes

For each unique index that is not a primary key, a special table is allocated that maps the unique key to the primary key of the indexed table. By default, an ordered index is also defined for each unique index. To prevent this, you must use the USING HASH option when defining the unique index. (See Chapter 1 for more detail on the USING HASH option.)

The default value of the MaxNoOfUniqueHashIndexes parameter is 64. Each index consumes approximately 15KB per node.

MaxNoOfTriggers

Internal update, insert, and delete triggers are allocated for each unique hash index. (This means that three triggers are created for each unique hash index.) However, an ordered index requires only a single trigger object. Backups also use three trigger objects for each normal table in the cluster.

The MaxNoOfTriggers parameter sets the maximum number of trigger objects in the cluster. The default value for this parameter is 768.

Boolean Parameters

The behavior of data nodes is affected by a set of parameters that take on Boolean values. You can specify these parameters as TRUE by setting them equal to 1 or Y and as FALSE by setting them equal to 0 or N.

LockPagesInMainMemory

For a number of operating systems, including Solaris and Linux, it is possible to lock a process into memory and so avoid any swapping to disk. You can use the LockPagesInMainMemory parameter to help guarantee the cluster's real-time characteristics.

By default, this feature is disabled. Of course, if you do this and then don't have enough RAM, you will have a problem (typically a node crash). You will also have no protection from a complete cluster shutdown; you will lose all your data and will have to restore from your last full backup. We don't recommend that you use this feature.

StopOnError

The StopOnError parameter specifies whether an ndbd process is to exit or to perform an automatic restart when an error condition is encountered. This feature is enabled by default.

You will notice that when you start ndbd, you get two processes. The "Angel" process restarts the "child" process when it meets an error condition if StopOnError is enabled. Otherwise, both processes exit (the default behavior).

Quite commonly, you will want to turn off this parameter, which makes the ndbd process attempt to restart automatically if they encounter an error. This is particularly useful in the event of a short-term network failure that may be fixed later on.

The drawback of setting this parameter is that, in theory, the data node may keep failing and restarting over and over, which could lead to overall cluster performance issues.

Diskless

It is possible to specify cluster tables as diskless, meaning that tables are not checkpointed to disk and that no logging occurs. Such tables exist only in main memory. A consequence of using diskless tables is that neither the tables nor the records in those tables will be preserved after a crash. However, when operating in diskless mode, it is possible to run ndbd on a diskless computer.

The ability to employ diskless mode on a per-table basis is planned for the 5.1 release of MySQL Cluster but is not currently supported.

Currently, when the Diskless parameter is enabled, backups are performed, but backup data is not actually stored (which makes the backups completely pointless).

Diskless is disabled by default, and we recommend that you not use it unless you are using diskless machines. Using it is very risky, and if your entire cluster shuts down, you *will* loose all your data (except for any traditional SQL backups you may have).

Controlling Timeouts, Intervals, and Disk Paging

A number of parameters specify timeouts and intervals between various actions in cluster data nodes. Most of the timeout values are specified in milliseconds.

TimeBetweenWatchDogCheck

To prevent the main ndbd thread from getting stuck in an endless loop, a "watchdog" thread checks the main thread. The TimeBetweenWatchDogCheck parameter specifies the number of milliseconds between checks. If the process remains in the same state after three checks, it is terminated by the watchdog thread.

The TimeBetweenWatchDogCheck parameter can easily be changed for purposes of experimentation or to adapt to local conditions. It can be specified on a per-node basis, although there seems to be little reason for doing so.

The default timeout is 4000 milliseconds (that is, 4 seconds).

StartPartialTimeout

The StartPartialTimeout parameter specifies the time that the cluster will wait for all storage nodes to come up before the cluster initialization routine is invoked. This timeout is used to avoid a partial cluster startup whenever possible.

The default value is 30000 milliseconds (that is, 30 seconds). 0 means eternal time out; in other words, the cluster may start only if all nodes are available.

StartPartitionedTimeout

If the cluster is ready to start after waiting for StartPartialTimeout milliseconds but is still in a possibly partitioned state (in other words, there is at least one node in each node group not yet connected), the cluster will wait this further period of time before starting. If it is not in a potentially partitioned state—for example, if all the nodes in one node group have connected—it will start immediately.

The default timeout is 60000 milliseconds (that is, 60 seconds).

StartFailureTimeout

If a storage node has not completed its startup sequence within the time specified by the StartFailureTimeout parameter, the node startup fails. If you set this parameter to 0, no data node timeout is applied, and nodes will continue to attempt to start eternally.

The default value is 60000 milliseconds (that is, 60 seconds). For data nodes that contain extremely large amounts of data, this parameter should be increased. For example, in the case of a storage node containing several gigabytes of data, a period as long as 10 to 15 minutes (that is, 600,000 to 1,000,000 milliseconds) might be required in order to perform a node start.

HeartbeatIntervalDbDb

One of the primary methods of discovering failed storage nodes is heartbeats. The HeartbeatIntervalDbDb parameter states how often heartbeat signals are sent and how often to expect to receive them. After missing three heartbeat intervals in a row, the node is declared dead. Thus the maximum time for discovering a failure through the heartbeat mechanism is four times the heartbeat interval.

The default heartbeat interval is 1500 milliseconds (that is, 1.5 seconds). This parameter must not be changed drastically and should not vary widely between nodes. If one node uses 5,000 milliseconds and the node watching it uses 1,000 milliseconds, obviously, the node will be declared dead very quickly. This parameter *can* be changed during an online software upgrade but only in small increments. (If half the nodes in the cluster are expecting to receive heartbeats every 1.5 seconds but you have changed the other half to send them every 15 seconds, you will get nodes thinking that other nodes are dead.)

HeartbeatIntervalDbApi

Each storage node sends heartbeat signals to each MySQL server (SQL node) to ensure that it remains in contact. If a MySQL server fails to send a heartbeat in time, it is declared dead, in which case all ongoing transactions are completed and all resources are released. The SQL node cannot reconnect until all activities started by the previous MySQL instance have been completed. The three-heartbeat criterion for the HeartbeatIntervalDbApi parameter is the same as that described for HeartbeatIntervalDbDb.

The default interval is again 1500 milliseconds (that is, 1.5 seconds). This interval can vary between individual storage nodes because each storage node watches the MySQL servers connected to it independently of all other storage nodes. However, again, there seems limited point in varying this, so we suggest that you define it in the DEFAULT section.

TimeBetweenLocalCheckpoints

The sizes of all write operations executed since the start of the previous local checkpoints are added together to decide whether nodes should start local checkpoints. The TimeBetweenLocalCheckpoints parameter specifies the minimum time between local checkpoints and can be used to prevent storage nodes in high-update/insert clusters starting the next local checkpoint immediately after the previous one has finished (independent of the cluster's workload). You can also use it to ensure that local checkpoints will follow each other with no gap (also independent of the cluster's workload) by setting it to 6 or less.

It should be noted that you are not actually setting a normal time in milliseconds, but you are specifying the base 2 logarithm of the number of 4-byte words of write operations that have built up since the last local checkpoint started, so that the default value 20 means 4MB $(4 \times (2^{20}))$ of write operations, 21 would mean 8MB, and so on, up to a maximum value of 31, which equates to 8GB of write operations.

> **Note**
> If you are wondering why it has been decided to set the `TimeBetweenLocalCheckpoints` parameter as it is set, you are not alone! You should get used to it, however, because defining a value in milliseconds would break your configuration because it would be far too large (2^{2000}, for example, if you were trying to mean 2 seconds).

TimeBetweenGlobalCheckpoints

When a transaction is committed, it is committed into the main memory (RAM) of all nodes on which the data is mirrored. However, transaction log records are not flushed to disk (hard drive) as part of the commit. The reasoning behind this behavior is that having the transaction safely committed on at least two autonomous host machines (in RAM) should meet reasonable standards for durability and is essential for good write/update performance. It means that during a complete cluster shutdown, you can technically loose a small number of fully committed transactions (the number depends on the value of this parameter).

It is also important to ensure that even the worst of cases—a complete crash of the cluster— is handled sensibly. To guarantee that this happens, all transactions taking place within a given interval are put into a global checkpoint, which can be thought of as a set of committed transactions that have been flushed to disk.

In other words, as part of the commit process, a transaction is placed in a global checkpoint group. Later on, this group's log records are flushed to disk, and then the entire group of transactions is safely committed to disk on all computers in the cluster as well.

The `TimeBetweenGlobalCheckpoints` parameter defines the interval between global checkpoints. The default is 2000 milliseconds (that is, 2 seconds). This means that in a worst-case scenario, you could lose up to 2 seconds of committed transactions from your cluster in the event of a total cluster shutdown the instant after the previous global checkpoint starts. If this is unacceptable to you, you should decrease the value of this parameter, but you need to realize that this will impose an extra load on your storage nodes.

TimeBetweenInactiveTransactionAbortCheck

Timeout handling is performed by checking a timer on each transaction once during every interval specified by the `TimeBetweenInactiveTransactionAbortCheck` parameter. Thus, if this parameter is set to 1000 milliseconds, every transaction will be checked for timing out once per second.

The default value for this parameter is 1000 milliseconds (that is, 1 second).

TransactionInactiveTimeout

If a transaction is currently not performing any queries but is waiting for further user input, the `TransactionInactiveTimeout` parameter states the maximum time that the user can wait before the transaction is aborted.

The default for this parameter is 0 (no timeout). For a real-time database that needs to ensure that no transaction keeps locks for too long a time, this parameter should be set to a small value, but not 0. The unit is milliseconds.

TransactionDeadlockDetectionTimeout

When a node executes a query involving an update or a write (in other words, creating a transaction), the node waits for the other nodes in the cluster to respond before continuing. A failure to respond can occur for any of the following reasons:

- The node is "dead."
- The operation has entered a lock queue.
- The node requested to perform the action is heavily overloaded.

The TransactionDeadlockDetectionTimeout parameter states how long the transaction coordinator will wait for query execution by another node before aborting the transaction, and this is important for both node failure handling and deadlock detection. Setting it too high can cause undesirable behavior in situations involving deadlocks and node failure.

The default timeout value is 1200 milliseconds (that is, 1.2 seconds).

NoOfDiskPagesToDiskAfterRestartTUP

When executing a local checkpoint, the storage nodes flush all data pages to disk. Merely doing this as quickly as possible without any moderation is likely to impose excessive loads on processors, networks, and disks. To control the write speed, the NoOfDiskPagesToDiskAfterRestartTUP parameter specifies how many pages per 100 milliseconds are to be written. In this context, a *page* is defined as 8KB; thus, this parameter is specified in units of 80KBps. Therefore, setting NoOfDiskPagesToDiskAfterRestartTUP to a value of 20 means writing 1.6MB of data pages to disk each second during a local checkpoint. Put simply, you should increase it if you want your local checkpoints to take less time but use more resources.

This value controls the writing of all data stored in DataMemory, so it includes the UNDO log records for data pages.

The default value is 40 (that is, 3.2MB of data pages per second).

NoOfDiskPagesToDiskAfterRestartACC

The NoOfDiskPagesToDiskAfterRestartACC parameter uses the same units as NoOfDiskPagesToDiskAfterRestartTUP (units of 80KB) and acts in a similar fashion, but it limits the speed of writing index pages from index memory.

The default value for this parameter is 20 index memory pages per second (that is, 1.6MBps).

NoOfDiskPagesToDiskDuringRestartTUP

The `NoOfDiskPagesToDiskDuringRestartTUP` parameter is similar to
`NoOfDiskPagesToDiskAfterRestartTUP` and `NoOfDiskPagesToDiskAfterRestartACC`, but it is
converted with local checkpoints executed on the node when a node is restarting. As part of
all node restarts, a local checkpoint is always performed. During a node restart, it is possible
to write to disk at a higher speed than at other times because fewer activities are being
performed in the node.

The default value is still 40 (that is, 3.2MBps), but we recommend that you increase this,
depending on the speed of your nodes.

NoOfDiskPagesToDiskDuringRestartACC

The `NoOfDiskPagesToDiskDuringRestartACC` parameter controls the number of index memory pages that can be written to disk during the local checkpoint phase of a node restart.

As with `NoOfDiskPagesToDiskAfterRestartTUP` and `NoOfDiskPagesToDiskAfterRestartACC`,
values for this parameter are expressed in terms of 8KB pages written per 100 milliseconds
(that is, 80KBps).

The default value is 20 (that is, 1.6MBps).

ArbitrationTimeout

The `ArbitrationTimeout` parameter specifies the time that the data node will wait for a
response from the arbitrator to an arbitration message. If this time is exceeded, it is assumed
that the network has split (and it will then carry out the relevant logic discussed in Chapter
1).

The default value is 1000 milliseconds (that is, 1 second).

Buffering

Buffers are used as front ends to the file system when writing log records to disk, to improve
performance (the storage nodes do not have to wait for the disk to catch up). If the node is
running in diskless mode, these parameters can be set to their minimum values without
penalty due to the fact that disk writes are "faked" (that is, they do not actually take place)
by the NDB storage engine's file system abstraction layer.

UndoIndexBuffer

The UNDO buffer is used during local checkpoints. The NDB storage engine uses a recovery
scheme based on checkpoint consistency in conjunction with an operational REDO log. Put
simply, it regularly takes a snapshot of the data in the cluster (local checkpoints), which it
does by applying the UNDO log to remove half-complete transactions[1] and then flushing the
resulting consistent copy of the database to disk. It also regularly stores the REDO log (which

contains the more recent transactions) to disk as part of the global checkpoint process. In the event of a failure, it applies the last known full commit to disk (local checkpoint) and then applies the REDO log (global checkpoint).

The UNDO index buffer is used to store updates on the primary key hash index. Inserts and deletions rearrange the hash index; the NDB storage engine writes UNDO log records that map all physical changes to an index page so that they can be undone at system restart. It also logs all active insert operations for each fragment at the start of a local checkpoint.

Reads and updates set lock bits and update a header in the hash index entry. These changes are handled by the page-writing algorithm to ensure that these operations need no UNDO logging.

The UndoIndexBuffer parameter is 2MB by default. The minimum value is 1MB, and for most applications, the minimum is sufficient. If your applications use extremely large and/or numerous insertions and deletions together with large transactions and large primary keys, it may be necessary to increase the size of this buffer. If this buffer is too small, the NDB storage engine issues internal error code 677: "Index UNDO buffers overloaded."

UndoDataBuffer

The UNDO data buffer plays the same role as the UNDO index buffer, except that it is used with regard to data memory rather than index memory. This buffer is used during the local checkpoint phase of a fragment for insertions, deletions, and updates.

Because UNDO log entries tend to grow larger as more operations are logged, the UndoDataBuffer parameter is typically set larger than its index memory counterpart, with a default value of 16MB.

For some applications, this amount of memory may be unnecessarily large. In such cases, it is possible to decrease this size down to a minimum of 1MB.

It is rarely necessary to increase the size of this buffer. If there is such a need, it is a good idea to check whether the disks can actually handle the load caused by database update activity. A lack of sufficient disk space or I/O capacity cannot be overcome by increasing the size of this buffer.

If this buffer is too small and gets congested, the NDB storage engine issues internal error code 891: "Data UNDO buffers overloaded."

RedoBuffer

All update activities need to be logged. The REDO log makes it possible to replay these updates whenever the system is restarted. The NDB recovery algorithm uses a "fuzzy"

---

1. By doing this, it does not have to prevent any writes during this process. The UNDO log is activated on one table fragment at a time.

checkpoint of the data together with the UNDO log, and then it applies the REDO log to play back all changes up to the restoration point.

The RedoBuffer parameter is 8MB by default. The minimum value is 1MB.

If this buffer is too small, the NDB storage engine issues error code 1221: "REDO log buffers overloaded."

Backup Parameters

The parameters discussed in the following sections define memory buffers set aside for execution of online backups.

BackupDataBufferSize

In creating a backup, there are two buffers used for sending data to the disk. The backup data buffer is used to fill in data recorded by scanning a node's tables. When this buffer has been filled to the level specified as BackupWriteSize (see the "BackupWriteSize" section), the pages are sent to disk. While flushing data to disk, the backup process can continue filling this buffer until it runs out of space. When this happens, the backup process pauses the scan and waits until some disk writes have completed and have thus freed up memory so that scanning may continue.

The default value for the BackupDataBufferSize parameter is 2MB.

BackupLogBufferSize

The backup log buffer fulfils a role similar to that played by the backup data buffer, except that it is used for generating a log of all table writes made during execution of the backup. The same principles apply for writing these pages as with the backup data buffer, except that when there is no more space in the backup log buffer, the backup fails. For that reason, the backup log buffer must be big enough to handle the load caused by write activities while the backup is being made.

The default value for the BackupLogBufferSize parameter should be sufficient for most applications. In fact, it is more likely for a backup failure to be caused by insufficient disk write speed than it is for the backup log buffer to become full. If the disk subsystem is not configured for the write load caused by applications, the cluster will be likely to be able to perform the desired operations.

It is preferable to configure cluster nodes in such a manner that the processor, rather than the disks or the network connections, becomes the bottleneck.

The default value is 2MB.

BackupWriteSize

The `BackupWriteSize` parameter specifies the size of messages written to disk by the backup log and backup data buffers.

The default value is `32KB`.

Logging

Some parameters are set as a level from 0 to 15, which determines how much information is sent to `stdout` (printed onscreen typically). The default is to send some (but not much) information about startup events to `stdout` and nothing else. Note that this is completely separate from the logging information covered earlier, in the section "`LogDestination`." This is information that affects only each individual storage node, although it makes sense to set the same values for all storage nodes the same (in other words, to set the value in the `DEFAULT` section).

LogLevelStartup

The `LogLevelStartup` parameter specifies the reporting level for events generated during startup of the process.

The default level is `1`.

LogLevelShutdown

The `LogLevelShutdown` parameter specifies the reporting level for events generated as part of graceful shutdown of a node.

The default level is `0`.

LogLevelStatistic

The `LogLevelStatistic` parameter specifies the reporting level for statistical events such as number of primary key reads, number of updates, number of inserts, information relating to buffer usage, and so on.

The default level is `0`.

LogLevelCheckpoint

The `LogLevelCheckpoint` parameter specifies the reporting level for events generated by local and global checkpoints.

The default level is `0`.

LogLevelNodeRestart

The LogLevelNodeRestart parameter specifies the reporting level for events generated during node restart.

The default level is 0.

LogLevelConnection

The LogLevelConnection parameter specifies the reporting level for events generated by connections between cluster nodes.

The default level is 0.

LogLevelError

The LogLevelError parameter specifies the reporting level for events generated by errors and warnings by the cluster as a whole. These errors do not cause any node failure but are still considered worth reporting.

The default level is 0.

LogLevelInfo

The LogLevelInfo parameter specifies the reporting level for events generated for information about the general state of the cluster.

The default level is 0.

Parameters to Define for Each Storage Node (NDBD)

Although you could set all the parameters we have looked at so far on a per-storage node basis, generally we suggest that it makes sense to have the same values for all nodes in the cluster and, therefore, unless there is a specific reason you want one node to have a different setting, we suggest that you just define all parameters in the [NDBD_DEFAULT] section.

This leaves the Id and Hostname parameters to set in each [NDBD] section.

An Example of a Storage Section of a config.ini File

Here is an example of a configuration with two storage nodes. It defines the parameters that most people will have to define, and this would make a good first configuration file to work from:

```
[NDBD DEFAULT]
# 2 replicas (min. for redundancy; requires 2 storage nodes min.)
NoOfReplicas=2
# Standard data directory
DataDir=/var/lib/mysql-cluster
```

```
# 512mb storage for data, 64mb for primary keys.
DataMemory=512mb
IndexMemory=64mb
# Define MaxNoOfConcurrentOperations; leave
# MaxNoOfLocalOperations as default (1.1*
# MaxNoOfConcurrentOperations)
MaxNoOfConcurrentOperations=10000
# Slightly increase the number of ordered indexes, unique hash
# indexes, tables and attributes allowed from defaults
# When importing tables, set this as high as you can
# Then reduce based on output from ALL DUMP 1000 command
MaxNoOfOrderedIndexes=512
MaxNoOfUniqueHashIndexes=256
MaxNoOfTables=256
MaxNoOfAttributes=1500

# 2 storage nodes
[NDBD]
# Allow auto allocation of ID, so just set hostname:
Hostname = 10.0.0.5

[NDBD]
Hostname = 10.0.0.6
```

Hopefully, you can see from this example how you would define the storage node section of your `config.ini` file, which is by far the largest and most important section.

Remember that if you change anything to do with the file system, you must restart the storage nodes by using the `--initial` parameter; the procedure for a cluster restart like this without any downtime is given at the beginning of this chapter, under the procedure for a rolling online configuration change.

SQL Nodes

SQL nodes can either be MySQL servers that connect to the cluster—which most are—or other cluster-specific binaries, such as the binaries described in Chapter 3, "Backup and Recovery."

Parameters to Define for All SQL Nodes (MYSQLD_DEFAULT)

We mention the following parameters for reference. It is unlikely that you are going to want to change them from the defaults. In addition, these only apply to SQL nodes that are MySQL servers connecting to the cluster—not to other binaries that may connect to the cluster.

ArbitrationRank

See the parameter with the same name in the section "Parameters to Define for All Management Nodes (NDB_MGMD_DEFAULT)." This parameter is identical to that one except that its default value is 2 (low priority).

ArbitrationDelay

Setting the ArbitrationDelay parameter to any other value than 0 (the default) means that responses by the arbitrator to arbitration requests will be delayed by the stated number of milliseconds. It is usually not necessary to change this value.

BatchByteSize

For queries that are translated into full table scans or range scans on indexes, it is important for best performance to fetch records in sensibly sized batches. It is possible to set the proper size both in terms of number of records (BatchSize) and in terms of bytes (BatchByteSize). The actual batch size is limited by both parameters (that is, it makes the batch as large as it can to be below both parameters).

The speed at which queries are performed can vary by more than 40%, depending on how the BatchByteSize parameter is set. In future releases, the MySQL server will make educated guesses on how to set parameters relating to batch size, based on the query type.

This parameter is measured in bytes and by default is equal to 32KB. If you have very fast hardware and good networking between nodes, you might want to increase this.

BatchSize

The BatchSize parameter is measured in terms of the number of records and is by default set to 64. The maximum size is 992. If you have very fast hardware and good networking between nodes, you might want to increase this.

MaxScanBatchSize

The batch size is the size of each batch sent from each storage node. Most scans are performed in parallel on the storage nodes, so in order to protect the MySQL server from receiving too much data from many nodes in parallel, the MaxScanBatchSize parameter sets a limit on the total batch size over all nodes. If your SQL nodes are not overloaded, you might want to increase this value significantly.

The default value of this parameter is set to 256KB. Its maximum size is 16MB.

Parameters to Define for Each SQL Node

As with storage nodes, you can set all the parameters that we suggest you put in the DEFAULT section in each individual SQL node part of the configuration file. If you have different hardware for different SQL nodes, we suggest that you do this. However, if you have identical hardware for all SQL nodes, there seems little point.

This leaves the Id and Hostname parameters to set in each [NDBD] section. We suggest that at the bottom of the SQL nodes section of your config.ini file, you leave a few SQL nodes with no Hostname so that you can connect extra cluster-related daemons from any host within your network. (When giving this advice, we assume that you have taken earlier advice and that your cluster is on a private network so there is no chance of anyone evil connecting to your cluster.) You will probably find this useful later on.

A Final Note on SQL Nodes

You should remember that if you are going to attempt to recover a backup, you need one SQL node per storage node available for the ndb_restore command to connect to. If you have followed our advice and have a few spare [MYSQLD] sections free with no Hostname defined, you should be able to do this without any changes.

Remember that there is no problem at all with specifying two SQL nodes with the same IP address. The first node ID will go to the first one to connect, and so on (you can specify which node is which with connectstrings, but we do not really see the point in doing so).

You should by now be familiar enough with producing configuration files that we do not give an example of a storage node section of a configuration file here. There is, however, a full config.ini example in the next section, "Using Multiple Management Nodes."

Using Multiple Management Nodes

To use multiple management nodes, first of all, you need to create a config.ini file, which must be the same (completely identical) for all management nodes (there is no checking done on this, but if the files are not identical, you will get a giant mess and a cluster crash). When using multiple management nodes, you have to assign all the IDs for the nodes manually in the configuration file. You cannot rely on auto-assignment due to the fact that you can have multiple management nodes assigning the IDs.

You then need to decide which of your management nodes is going to be primary. For example, say that the primary management node is 10.0.1.0, and the backup is 10.0.1.1. Assume a storage and SQL node each on 10.0.1.2 and 10.0.1.3:

```
[NDB_MGMD DEFAULT]
PortNumber=1186
LogDestination=CONSOLE;SYSLOG:facility=syslog;FILE:filename=/var/log/cluster-log
DataDir=/var/lib/mysql-cluster
ArbitrationRank=1

# First (PRIMARY) mgm node
[NDB_MGMD]
Id = 1
Hostname = 10.0.1.0
```

```
# Second (BACKUP) mgm node
[NDB_MGMD]
Id = 2
Hostname = 10.0.1.1

# Storage nodes
[NDBD_DEFAULT]
DataDir=/var/lib/mysql-cluster
[NDBD]
Id=3
Hostname=10.0.1.2
[NDBD]
Id=4
Hostname=10.0.1.3

#SQL Nodes
[MYSQLD]
Id=5
Hostname=10.0.1.2
[MYSQLD]
Id=6
Hostname=10.0.1.3
```

Now, on all four servers, you place the following in /etc/my.cnf:

```
[mysqld]
ndbcluster
#connectstring: primary,secondary management nodes
ndb-connectstring=10.0.0.0,10.0.0.1
[mysql_cluster]
ndb-connectstring=id=x,10.0.0.0,10.0.0.1
```

Notice the id=x in the second connectstring: Make sure you put the correct node ID (as specified in the configuration file) in here.

Now, on the primary management server, you start ndb_mgmd as per the instructions in Chapter 1, in the section "Starting a Management Node." Once it is started, you switch to the secondary management server and start ndb_mgmd there exactly as before. Finally, you start the two storage nodes (ndbd) and restart MySQL on the two SQL nodes. You should see something like this:

```
ndb_mgm> SHOW
Connected to Management Server at: 10.0.0.0:1186
Cluster Configuration
---------------------
[ndbd(NDB)]     2 node(s)
id=3    @10.0.0.2  (Version: 5.0.12, Nodegroup: 0)
id=4    @10.0.0.3  (Version: 5.0.12, Nodegroup: 0, Master)
```

```
[ndb_mgmd(MGM)]  2 node(s)
id=1    (Version: 5.0.12)
id=2    (Version: 5.0.12)

[mysqld(API)]    4 node(s)
id=5    @10.0.0.2  (Version: 5.0.12)
id=6    @10.0.0.3  (Version: 5.0.12)
```

> **Note**
>
> Note that 10.0.1.0 is the IP address of the primary management daemon. If you use ndb_mgm on any of the four servers (including the server that is running the backup ndb_mgmd daemon), you should still get this output: It should connect to the primary because at this stage the primary is working.

Now, let's see what happens when you unplug the power cable to the primary management daemon, 10.0.0.0. First of all, you should start ndb_mgm on one of the other three server (that is, not the one that you are going to unplug). Then you unplug the server that the primary management daemon is running on. Next, try to run a SHOW command:

```
ndb_mgm> SHOW
Could not get status
*      0: No error
*        Executing: ndb_mgm_disconnect
```

It appears not to have worked. But this is what you expected; the management client is still trying to talk to the *primary* management daemon. If you exit and reopen ndb_mgm, it should work:

```
ndb_mgm> exit
[root@s1 mysql-cluster]# ndb_mgm
-- NDB Cluster -- Management Client --
ndb_mgm> show;
Connected to Management Server at: 10.0.0.1:1186
Cluster Configuration
---------------------
[ndbd(NDB)]     2 node(s)
id=3    @10.0.0.2  (Version: 5.0.12, Nodegroup: 0)
id=4    @10.0.0.3  (Version: 5.0.12, Nodegroup: 0, Master)

[ndb_mgmd(MGM)] 2 node(s)
id=1 (not connected, accepting connect from 10.0.0.0)
id=2    @10.0.0.1  (Version: 5.0.12)
```

```
[mysqld(API)]    4 node(s)
id=5    (Version: 5.0.12)
id=6    (Version: 5.0.12)
```

> **Note**
> Note that you are now on the IP address of the backup management node.

The NDB and API nodes do *not* need to be restarted in the event of a primary management daemon failure. They will start communicating with the backup management daemon almost immediately, and they will switch back as and when they need to.

Backup and Recovery

Backups and the recovery process are a very important topic for a database management system. Backups act as the last line of defense if everything else goes wrong. There are two possible causes of these catastrophic events. The first is a user-induced failure, in which a user accidentally or maliciously affects your data in a negative way. An example would be if someone issued DROP TABLE or DELETE to remove data. The only way to recover in the event of such an action would be to use a backup. The second possible cause of a catastrophic data loss is if you have simultaneous hardware failures on all the members of a node group. For example, if all the node groups suffer a hard drive corruption/failure, there won't be data available to recover from. Generally, to mitigate the danger from these events occurring, you should make backups quite frequently (normally at least once per day, if not more frequently).

You may also need to do a backup and recover from it if you are upgrading or changing a system setting. Many upgrades and configuration changes can be online, but some cannot be. The configuration parameters that require a backup/recovery process are ones that affect the partitioning of the data, including NoOfReplicas, as well as those that change the number of data nodes in the cluster. As far as software upgrades are concerned, generally minor updates (for example, from version 5.0.12 to version 5.0.13) can be done in an online manner through a rolling upgrade process (as explained in Chapter 1, "Installation"). Major version upgrades (for example, from version 4.1 to version 5.0) also require a backup/restore in order to proceed.

MySQL Cluster's Native Backup Tool

MySQL Cluster includes a native backup tool that allows you to make online backups. This is the most common tool to use for backups because it allows normal continuous running of the cluster while you're making the backup, as it doesn't set any locks to make the backup. The native backup tool only backs up those database objects that are clustered (for example, table structures and data). This tool does not back up objects such as databases, stored procedures, and triggers, so you need to back them up by using some other method.

To control MySQL Cluster's native backup tool, you use the management client, ndb_mgm. There are two commands related to dealing with the back process: START BACKUP and ABORT BACKUP. To initiate the backup process, you use the START BACKUP command. You can use a few options with this command to control when the command will return. The default is WAIT COMPLETED, which causes the command to wait until all the nodes have successfully reported that the backup was complete. If you have a lot of data in the cluster, this command may take a long time to complete, so it might be better to use one of the other options. WAIT STARTED causes the command to wait until all the nodes have successfully received the command to start making a backup and actually start the process. The final option is the NOWAIT option, which causes the command to return immediately, without waiting for the data nodes to confirm that they have started or finished. The following are some examples of these commands:

```
shell> ndb_mgm -e "START BACKUP NOWAIT"
ndb_mgm> START BACKUP WAIT COMPLETED
Waiting for completed, this may take several minutes
Node 2: Backup 2 started from node 1
Node 2: Backup 2 started from node 1 completed
 StartGCP: 114086 StopGCP: 114089
 #Records: 5321 #LogRecords: 0
 Data: 191220 bytes Log: 0 bytes
```

Regardless of the option you use to initiate a backup, the cluster log will contain information about the backup process as well. You can monitor this log if you have used the NOWAIT option to see when it completes. The cluster log file has output similar to the following:

```
2005-11-25 17:02:42 [MgmSrvr] INFO     -- Node 2: Backup 1 started from node 1
2005-11-25 17:02:43 [MgmSrvr] INFO     -- Node 2: Backup 1 started from node 1
 completed
 StartGCP: 114078 StopGCP: 114081
 #Records: 5321 #LogRecords: 0
 Data: 191220 bytes Log: 0 bytes
2005-11-25 17:02:53 [MgmSrvr] INFO     -- Node 2: Backup 2 started from node 1
2005-11-25 17:02:53 [MgmSrvr] INFO     -- Node 2: Backup 2 started from node 1
 completed
 StartGCP: 114086 StopGCP: 114089
 #Records: 5321 #LogRecords: 0
 Data: 191220 bytes Log: 0 bytes
```

Notice that each backup you make is assigned a number, called the backup ID. It is important to know this ID when you want to use a backup later on for recovery. If you don't have the number, it isn't too important because you can get it from the name of the backup. The backup ID numbers increment, so the largest number is the most recent backup. The incrementing number persists across cluster restarts, but an all --initial restart resets the number. You need to be careful if you reset it in this manner because it will overwrite the previous backups if they still exist in the same location when you try to make a new backup.

The backup itself is stored locally on the hard drive of each data node. For example, if you have four data nodes, four locations contain the data required to restore your backup. You normally have to copy all these files into a single location in order to store your backup for the long term. MySQL Cluster doesn't have a built-in way to do this, but it should be fairly trivial to do it by using something such as scp or rsync. Chapter 4, "Security and Management," provides some examples of scripts to do similar things.

The backup itself is stored in a directory called BACKUP. Normally, this is inside the DataDir defined in the cluster configuration file. However, it is possible to move it with an additional cluster configuration option called BackupDataDir. Each backup you make creates an additional directory within this BACKUP directory called BACKUP-#, where # is the backup ID. Inside the BACKUP-# directory are three files—BACKUP-#.N.ctl, BACKUP-#.N.log, and BACKUP-#-M.N.Data—where # is the backup ID, N is the node ID of the originating node, and M is the file number. The .ctl file is the metadata from the cluster. This includes information about what tables, indexes, triggers, and so on exist. The second set of files is the .Data files, which contain the data from your entire system. In theory, there can be multiple .Data files, depending on how much data is in your system. The final file is the .log file. This is the UNDO log used to make the backup consistent, and it allows the backup to not set any locks while occurring. It is automatically reapplied during system recovery. Your BACKUP directory should look similar to the following:

```
shell:~/ndb/BACKUP/BACKUP-1$ ls -l
total 432
-rw-r-----   1 user   group   99568 Nov 25 17:19 BACKUP-1-0.2.Data
-rw-r-----   1 user   group   91956 Nov 25 17:19 BACKUP-1-0.3.Data
-rw-r-----   1 user   group    6384 Nov 25 17:19 BACKUP-1.2.ctl
-rw-r-----   1 user   group      44 Nov 25 17:19 BACKUP-1.2.log
-rw-r-----   1 user   group    6384 Nov 25 17:19 BACKUP-1.3.ctl
-rw-r-----   1 user   group      44 Nov 25 17:19 BACKUP-1.3.log
```

The other management client command involved in backups is the ABORT BACKUP # command. This command allows you to stop a backup that is in progress. It causes the data nodes to delete all the data that has to that point been written out as well. This command does not return an error if the backup isn't in progress, even though it doesn't do anything because there is nothing to abort. If the abort occurs, you see a message in the cluster log confirming that it was aborted:

```
ndb_mgm> ABORT BACKUP 2
Abort of backup 2 ordered
```

In the cluster log you see this:

```
2005-11-25 18:13:47 [MgmSrvr] INFO     -- Node 3: Backup 5 started from node 1
2005-11-25 18:13:47 [MgmSrvr] ALERT    -- Node 3: Backup 5 started from 1 has
been aborted. Error: 1321
```

Using `mysqldump` for Backups

Another way you can make backups is by using a tool called `mysqldump`. If you have been using MySQL with other storage engines, this tool should be familiar to you. Using `mysqldump` to back up non-cluster objects, such as triggers and stored procedures, works exactly the same as with non-clustered databases. Quite commonly when doing this, you should use the `--no-data` flag with `mysqldump` to ensure that you aren't backing up clustered data. If you want to use it to back up clustered data, you need to follow a few special restrictions related to using it with MySQL Cluster. The special restrictions exist because MySQL Cluster doesn't have a repeatable read isolation level and doesn't support distributed table locking (the two methods used by `mysqldump` for making consistent backups). Generally, you use `mysqldump` only if you needed to restore the data into a different system (that is, not into MySQL Cluster).

If you want to back up data with `mysqldump` in order for `mysqldump` to get a consistent view of the data, you need to enter single-user mode before making the backup (or otherwise ensure that no one else is going to be changing data while you're making the backup). This allows `mysqldump` to get a consistent view of the data to backup. However, this will not be an online backup because users will be denied access to the cluster while this is continuing.

After you enter single-user mode, you can make a backup as you normally would. There are many different options you can use with `mysqldump` to change the format and other parameters. We recommend that you take a look at the output of `mysqldump --help` and at the webpage for `mysqldump` (http://dev.mysql.com/doc/refman/5.0/en/mysqldump.html), which includes many examples. You should make sure to use one of the backup methods that lock the tables first, such as the `--lock-tables` option or the `--master-data` option. With `mysqldump`, you can choose what pieces to back up as well, whereas the native hot backup tool always does all the data for all tables.

The following is an example of a `mysqldump` command to back up the `world` database data while in single-user mode:

```
shell> mysqldump -u root -p --lock-tables world > backup-world.sql
```

Single-User Mode

Single-user mode allows you to lock down a cluster so that it is accessible only to a single MySQL server (or similar connection to the cluster). All other servers give an error when someone tries to access one of the tables stored in the cluster.

To enter single-user mode, you issue the command ENTER SINGLE USER MODE #, where # is the node ID of the node you want to allow to communicate with the cluster. Entering this mode can take a brief time to complete; you can see when you have entered single-user mode by using the ALL STATUS command or the SHOW command. When you are done with the mode, you can use the command EXIT SINGLE USER MODE to resume normal operation.

The following is an example of a session:

```
ndb_mgm> ENTER SINGLE USER MODE 4
Entering single user mode
Access will be granted for API node 4 only.
Use ALL STATUS to see when single user mode has been entered.
ndb_mgm> ALL STATUS
Node 2: single user mode (Version 5.0.13)
Node 3: single user mode (Version 5.0.13)

ndb_mgm> SHOW
Cluster Configuration
---------------------
[ndbd(NDB)]     2 node(s)
id=2    @127.0.0.1  (Version: 5.0.13, single user mode, Nodegroup: 0)
id=3    @127.0.0.1  (Version: 5.0.13, single user mode, Nodegroup: 0, Master)

[ndb_mgmd(MGM)] 1 node(s)
id=1    @127.0.0.1  (Version: 5.0.13)

[mysqld(API)]   2 node(s)
id=4    @127.0.0.1  (Version: 5.0.13)
id=5 (not connected, accepting connect from any host)

ndb_mgm> EXIT SINGLE USER MODE
Exiting single user mode in progress.
Use ALL STATUS to see when single user mode has been exited.
ndb_mgm> ALL STATUS
Node 2: started (Version 5.0.13)
Node 3: started (Version 5.0.13)
```

Single-user mode is useful for a few different things. First, it is somewhat like `mysqldump`, as mentioned previously. Second, it is useful when you're restoring a backup into MySQL Cluster. When you restore a backup (either from `mysqldump` or by using the hot backup method), you should normally enter single-user mode. In this way, restoring a backup is not a hot operation. Finally, there are some maintenance tasks for which you generally want to enter single-user mode as well. This includes tasks such as ALTER TABLE, which need to be synchronized across all the MySQL servers.

The following is a typical example of the usage of this mode in order to ensure you make a consistent backup of the `world` database:

```
shell> ndb_mgm -e "ENTER SINGLE USER MODE 4"; sleep 10;
        mysqldump -u root -p --lock-tables world > backup-world.sql;
        ndb_mgm -e "EXIT SINGLE USER MODE";
```

Restoring a Backup

The previous sections cover how to perform a backup operation. But a backup is useless if you cannot properly recover from it. The recovery process is relatively simple for both of the backup methods discussed. However, you should generally practice the process a few times before you attempt to do it on a production system.

Restoring a Backup by Using Native Hot Backup

To restore a backup made by using the native hot backup tool, you use the ndb_restore program that comes with the MySQL Cluster installation. This program reads the backup files and loads the data and structure into a running cluster. The cluster that the data is being loaded into can have a different topography than the original cluster. For example, if you want to increase from two data nodes to four data nodes, you can do it without any problems when you use this backup method.

ndb_restore connects to the cluster in the same manner as a MySQL server does, and then it effectively re-issues the CREATE and INSERT statements needed to re-create your tables. Because it connects directly to the cluster, you need to make sure you have an extra [mysqld] section in your cluster configuration file for it. You still need to manually re-create your databases and other non-clustered objects after you restore this backup.

These are the steps for restoring a backup taken by the native hot backup:

1. Enter single-user mode for the node ID you plan to use for ndb_restore (or otherwise guarantee that no one else is using the cluster).
2. From within the BACKUP-# directory, use the ndb_restore tool to restore the metadata (that is, table structure) of the system by using -m or --restore_meta.
3. Use ndb_restore to restore the data from the fragment to the tables, with the -r or --restore_data option.
4. Repeat step 3 for each of the other data nodes. (For example, if you had four data nodes when you made the backup, you need to perform step 3 four times.)
5. Leave single-user mode. Your cluster is now ready to be used.

When using ndb_restore, you are required to specify a few options.

- **-b or -backupid**—You use this option to specify the backup ID that needs to be restored. The backup ID is the number immediately after the BACKUP word. For example, with BACKUP-7.2.ctl, the backup ID is 7.
- **The original node ID for the backup**—Again, you can get this ID from the filename; it is the number listed immediately before the file extension. For example, with BACKUP-7.2.ctl, the original node ID is 2.
- **-m, -r, or both**—You use these options to specify whether to restore the schema, the data, or both at the same time.

The following is an example of a session involving restoring from a native backup of two nodes

```
shell:~/ndb/BACKUP/BACKUP-1$ ls -l
total 432
-rw-r-----   1 user   group  99568 Nov 25 17:19 BACKUP-1-0.2.Data
-rw-r-----   1 user   group  91956 Nov 25 17:19 BACKUP-1-0.3.Data
-rw-r-----   1 user   group   6384 Nov 25 17:19 BACKUP-1.2.ctl
-rw-r-----   1 user   group     44 Nov 25 17:19 BACKUP-1.2.log
-rw-r-----   1 user   group   6384 Nov 25 17:19 BACKUP-1.3.ctl
-rw-r-----   1 user   group     44 Nov 25 17:19 BACKUP-1.3.log
shell:~/ndb/BACKUP/BACKUP-1$ ndb_restore -m -b 1 -n 2
Ndb version in backup files: Version 5.0.13
Connected to ndb!!
Successfully restored table world/def/countrylanguage
Successfully restored table world/def/country
Successfully created index PRIMARY on countrylanguage
Successfully created index PRIMARY on country

NDBT_ProgramExit: 0 - OK


shell:~/ndb/BACKUP/BACKUP-1$ ndb_restore -r -b 1 -n 2
Ndb version in backup files: Version 5.0.13
Connected to ndb!!
_____

Processing data in table: world/def/countrylanguage(3) fragment 0
_____

Processing data in table: world/def/country(2) fragment 0
_____

Processing data in table: sys/def/NDB$EVENTS_0(1) fragment 0
_____

Processing data in table: sys/def/SYSTAB_0(0) fragment 0
Restored 627 tuples and 0 log entries

NDBT_ProgramExit: 0 - OK


shell:~/ndb/BACKUP/BACKUP-1$ ndb_restore -r -b 1 -n 3
Ndb version in backup files: Version 5.0.13
Connected to ndb!!
_____

Processing data in table: world/def/countrylanguage(3) fragment 1
_____

Processing data in table: world/def/country(2) fragment 1
_____

Processing data in table: sys/def/NDB$EVENTS_0(1) fragment 1
```

```
Processing data in table: sys/def/SYSTAB_0(0) fragment 1
Restored 596 tuples and 0 log entries

NDBT_ProgramExit: 0 - OK
```

Restoring a Backup Made Using `mysqldump`

To restore a backup made by using `mysqldump`, you simply redirect the file you saved the output to into the `mysql` command-line client. This causes the client to reissue all the SQL commands needed to restore your database objects and data (if you made a backup of the data). Generally, you need to make sure the cluster isn't in use when you are doing this.

You need to log in to the MySQL server by using normal user account privileges (normally as the root user with a password).

The following is an example of this command:

```
shell> mysql -u root -p < file.sql
```

If the command returns, you know the backup has completed successfully. If it gives an error, something has gone wrong (possibly version incompatibilities or something similar).

Keep in mind that if this restoration is creating non-clustered objects, such as stored procedures and triggers, you need to follow this procedure on each MySQL server to restore them all fully. Chapter 4 provides some examples of scripts you can use as a basis to do this easily.

When doing this type of restoration, you might want to consider setting the MySQL server variable `ndb_use_transactions` to `false` or `off`. This allows you to not have any problems with `REDO` log segments.

Speeding Up Restoration

When restoring data, the biggest thing you can do to attempt to speed things up is to do the restoration in parallel. Because a cluster has many data nodes, you generally want to do many loads at the same time to take advantage of them and to avoid bottlenecks such as network bottlenecks.

With native backups, this is quite easy because the data for your tables is split into many files (one for each data node). You can simply restore the metadata from one and then restore the data from all the nodes at the same time. The exact number of restorations to do at once depends on the number of data nodes you have, network settings, and so on. We recommend that you do some simple testing to determine the ideal number of restorations to do at once. Keep in mind that each `ndb_restore` running at once requires its own `[mysqld]` slot in the cluster configuration.

Getting the load to occur in parallel with `mysqldump` takes a bit of effort. We recommend possibly splitting each table into a different dump file and then loading it in that way. If you are just dumping a single database, you can use the `--tab` option for `mysqldump` to produce a separate file for each table, which can then possibly make it easier to load in parallel.

Troubleshooting Backups

There are a few reasons the MySQL Cluster native backup tool may fail to make a backup. The following sections discuss a few common problems and how to solve them.

If a problem occurs while making a backup, it should always be reported in the cluster log. It is a good practice to monitor the cluster log for any such issues. The cluster log should give a general idea as to why the backup failed. It might be because someone manually aborted the backup by using the `ABORT BACKUP` command or be due to an uncontrollable cause, such as the three mentioned in the following sections.

In the unlikely event that the backup causes a node to fail, you can find more information in the node log and also in the trace file for the node that failed.

Disk Is Full

If you get a "disk is full" error, you need to ensure that the backup has enough space to complete. To solve this problem, you can either free up space or move `BackupDataDir` to some place that has more space.

Disk Is Too Slow

If the disk to which you are making a backup isn't fast enough, the backup might fail. A system of two different memory buffers is used when you make a backup. The first one is `BackupDataBufferSize`, which is used for buffering data before it is written to disk. The second one, which is important for this error, is `BackupLogBufferSize`. This is the buffer that is used to record data changes before writing to disk. If this buffer ever fills up due to the disk not being able to keep up with the number of changes occurring during the backup, the backup will fail. If that occurs, you can either attempt to increase this buffer or move the backup to be taken to a faster disk subsystem.

Not Enough Memory

As mentioned previously, some additional memory sections are allocated when performing a backup. If your system is too low on resources, this memory allocation can fail, which causes the cluster in MySQL Cluster to abort the backup process.

In order to fix this, you should either decrease the sizes of `BackupDataBufferSize` and `BackupLogBufferSize` or decrease another memory parameter in order to allow sufficient space for these to be allocated.

4

Security and Management

The first section of this chapter, which discusses security, does not strictly relate to MySQL Cluster. That is, there is very little here that users experienced with Linux security will find new, and such users can either skim or skip this section and go straight to the "Managing MySQL Cluster" section, later in this chapter. However, many database administrators will suddenly find that they need to learn how to secure a cluster in MySQL Cluster, and this chapter will help them. It covers what you have to do to secure a cluster, and it does not expect any significant previous knowledge of Linux security.

This chapter covers Linux security in step-by-step detail; you should be able to transfer this information onto other platforms, if needed.

Security for MySQL Cluster

MySQL Cluster is an inherently insecure system: It has no security whatsoever built into it. If you have followed along with the examples so far in this book, anyone with even the most basic knowledge could connect to your cluster and steal or sabotage your data.

The first important thing to do in implementing security with MySQL Cluster is to separate any traffic within your cluster from any traffic coming in from outside. You can do this by using firewalls, which control what packets can pass through them on the basis of some simple rules or you can separate MySQL Cluster traffic onto a different network that is physically separate from your public network and therefore secure.

MySQL Cluster requires *significant* numbers of ports to be open for communication intern-ode, which is why we suggest that you use a totally separate network for cluster traffic. It is then easy to prevent the forwarding of traffic from one network to the other, and you have then achieved the first goal.

You should be aware that currently there is no checking of the source IP address for ndb_mgm clients, so anyone who has access to port 1186 on the management daemon can download a copy of ndb_mgm, connect to your management daemon, and do just about anything (for example, shut down the cluster). Clearly, this is not acceptable. Three different network designs eliminate this risk: The most preferable is also most expensive, although one solution is inexpensive and relies purely on software protection, with a third option available which is a mix of the other two.

Figure 4.1 shows the best possible scenario for your cluster, with separate public and private networks.

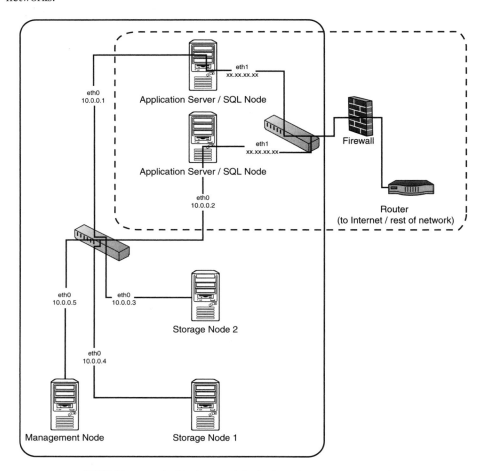

FIGURE 4.1   An ideal network for both performance and security.

The network in Figure 4.1 has two completely separate networks: the private network (solid box) and the public network (dashed box). For performance reasons, we suggest that you use a gigabit switch for the private network because cluster nodes can transfer enormous amounts of data between each other during the normal course of operations. You can see that there is now no way for someone sitting on the public network to access the data that is traveling between cluster nodes on the private network without going through either of the application servers. In other words, internal cluster traffic (for example, from Storage Node 1 to Storage Node 2 or from App Server 1 to Storage Node 2) is completely segregated, which is excellent.

Notice in Figure 4.1 how the local network is using local addresses. We suggest that you use local addresses for your cluster nodes if they are on a separate network (we have done so in this book). This is primarily for clarity rather than security. You can choose from one of the following three sets of reserved IP addresses:

10.0.0.0–10.255.255.255
172.16.0.0–172.31.255.255
192.168.0.0–192.168.255.255

If the application servers are set so that they do not allow any forwarding (which they will be by default), and if they are themselves not hacked, your cluster data is safe from sniffing and interference. Of course, sniffing and interference are not the only threats to your cluster by any stretch of the imagination, but they are the major threats that you are much more vulnerable to if you run a cluster in MySQL Cluster when compared to a standard MySQL server due to the volumes of plain-text information moved around between nodes and the complete lack of any form of authentication or security.

This means you still need to secure your application servers against hackers, as you normally would. (Such securing is beyond the scope of this book. However, we do cover setting up software firewalls, in the context of what you have to allow for the cluster to continue to work, in the section "Software Firewalls," later in this chapter.) You can be more restrictive with your firewall rules. For example, if your application servers are only running a web service, you can block all traffic coming in on eth0 except to 80 (and 443, if you are running SSL, and 22 if you need SSH).

If you are unable to set up two separate networks, you should make sure your network is partitioned as far as possible, ideally with all your cluster nodes plugged in to a switch, which is then plugged in to a router to keep all internal traffic in your network away from any other computers in the network. If you can get a hardware firewall, you can implement the second-best setup (in terms of both security and performance), as shown in Figure 4.2. (It is recommended even more strongly in this case that your switch be a gigabit switch.)

The setup shown in Figure 4.2 requires the hardware firewall to follow a simple rule that says something like this: "Deny all traffic except to the two application servers on the ports that whatever application requires for clients to connect to it."

This may seem unclear, so let's consider an example: "Ports that whatever application requires" would be 80 for HTTP, 443 for SSL, 3306 for MySQL client access, and so on. In other words, you could only allow ports that are actually required for your end users to connect to the servers, and this depends on what application your end users are connecting to.

Such a firewall should also filter egress traffic, again denying all traffic except traffic that is specifically required for the application to run.

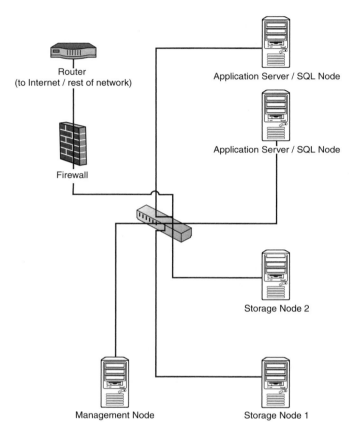

FIGURE 4.2   The second-best network setup in terms of security and performance.

If you do not have access to a hardware firewall, then security can become very difficult, and you will have to be very careful with your software firewalls. To start with, you should be very careful with your network partitioning to make sure that malicious elements can't either sniff data traveling between nodes in your cluster or, worse, modify it with spoofed packets. Many routers incorporate features that can block both of these forms of attack; it is certainly worth making sure that yours are configured to do so and that ideally your cluster is on a dedicated network segment.

In a typical cluster, you will be left with two "zones" of nodes, as shown in Figure 4.3.

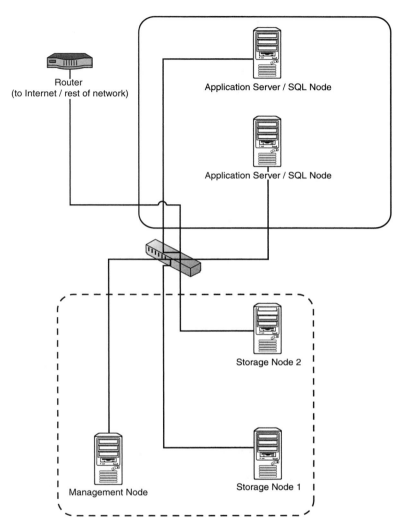

FIGURE 4.3   Two "zones" of nodes that require protection
with software firewalls.

Figure 4.3 shows the storage and management nodes in one zone (dotted box). These nodes need to be able to communicate with each other and communicate with the SQL nodes. The figure also shows a zone that contains the application servers (solid box). These nodes need to be able to communicate with the users of your application and communicate with the storage nodes.

It is essential that the users of the application are *not* able to communicate with the storage and management nodes directly. Otherwise, malicious traffic could bring down your cluster. You therefore need to be very careful with your software firewalls, and you need to block everything that is not necessary as discussed in the next section.

Software Firewalls

This section covers the most restrictive firewall ruleset possible for the sample cluster shown in Figure 4.3. It explains what rules you want, and then it shows the exact configuration required for an APF firewall.

For the application nodes, you want rules that operate like this:

- DENY all traffic unless
  - It comes from a management or storage node (any port; TCP or UDP)

> **Note**
> It is possible to define exactly what ports each node will actually use, but there seems little point.

  - It comes from the rest of the network *and* it is on port 80 (TCP, assuming that your application is running HTTP; change this to whatever your application is running)

> **Note**
> We assume at this stage that you are actually running your application on the application servers in Figure 4.3 (that is, that they are running SQL nodes and the application is connecting to localhost). This is the most standard way of doing it, but you can of course put your application on a separate set of servers and have them connect to a MySQL server on 3306 running on the application servers in Figure 4.3.

For the storage nodes, you want rules that work like this:

- DENY all traffic unless
  - It comes from another management or storage node (any port; TCP or UDP)
  - It comes from an application server *and* is on port 1186 (TCP or UDP)

Linux is blessed with many excellent software firewalls. The ones most commonly used are based on a package called `iptables`. `iptables` is itself a development of an older and in its own time very popular system called `ipchains` (which itself was based on a package called `ipfw` for BSD).

However, `iptables` is rather complex to configure directly, and we suggest that you use a program called APF to configure your firewall, particularly if you are new to Linux software firewalls, because APF produces the correct `iptables` rules for you based on a simple-to-understand configuration file. APF also has several modules that make it an excellent choice as a firewall, including brute force detection (which is essential for any Internet-facing server with SSH or any other interface enabled) as well as advanced denial of service mitigation. APF is released under the General Public License and is completely free.

Installing and Configuring an `IPTables`-Based Firewall

`IPTables` is installed by default on almost all Linux distributions. It operates as a set of rules, and every time the Linux kernel receives or wants to send a packet, it runs through the rules until it finds one that matches the packet and defines what to do with it. If it does not find a rule that matches the packet, the fate of the packet is determined by the default action, which is typically `DROP`.

APF has a very simple configuration file that sets the global options and then there are two extra files—one that specifies traffic that you certainly want to get rid of (drop) and one that specifies traffic that you certainly want to allow.

The following sections show how to set up servers to disallow all traffic except SSH on all nodes from a certain IP address and web traffic on port 80 to the application nodes.

Downloading and Installing APF

APF is released as a `tar` package that you must untar and install. However, it does not require compiling, and the installation process is very simple, as shown here:

```
[user@host] su -
Enter Password:
[root@host] cd /usr/src/
[root@host] wget http://www.rfxnetworks.com/downloads/apf-current.tar.gz
--12:49:19--  http://www.rfxnetworks.com/downloads/apf-current.tar.gz
           => `apf-current.tar.gz'
Resolving www.rfxnetworks.com... 67.15.39.216
Connecting to www.rfxnetworks.com[67.15.39.216]:80... connected.
HTTP request sent, awaiting response... 200 OK
Length: 82,187 [application/x-gzip]

100%[====================================>] 82,187        57.39K/s
```

```
12:49:22 (57.30 KB/s) - `apf-current.tar.gz' saved [82,187/82,187]

[root@host] tar -xvzf apf-current.tar.gz
apf-0.9.5-1/
(output from tar command here)

[root@host] cd apf*
[root@host] ./install.sh
Installing APF 0.9.5-1: Completed.

Installation Details:
  Install path:        /etc/apf/
  Config path:         /etc/apf/conf.apf
  Executable path:     /usr/local/sbin/apf
  AntiDos install path: /etc/apf/ad/
  AntiDos config path:  /etc/apf/ad/conf.antidos
  DShield Client Parser: /etc/apf/extras/dshield/

Other Details:
  Listening TCP ports: 111,631,1024,1186,3306
  Listening UDP ports: 68,111,631,804,1024
  Note: These ports are not auto-configured; they are simply presented
  for information purposes. You must manually configure all port options.
[root@host]
```

Congratulations! You have installed APF. However, by default, APF will disable itself every 5 minutes (this is in case you deny access to SSH from your IP address by mistake and lock yourself out). You also need to configure it in a bit more detail, as described in the following section.

Configuring APF

You now need to configure the main configuration APF file: /etc/apf/conf.apf. This file contains settings such as what ports are open to all source IP addresses and whether to filter egress (outgoing) traffic.

The following lines are the ones you are likely to be interested in:

- IG_TCP_CPORTS="22"—You want to make this IG_TCP_CPORTS="22,80" on your application servers to allow web traffic in. (You should leave it alone for all servers not running your application; clearly, if your application is not running on port 80 (HTTP), you should put in the correct port.) Also, if you are going to only allow SSH traffic in from one IP address or a class of IP addresses, you want to remove 22 here and add it later to the allow_hosts.rules file.

- **EGF="0"**—This is where you set whether you filter outgoing traffic (1=yes). This is not a bad idea and makes life a little bit harder for any malicious users who may attempt to take control of your server.
- **EG_TCP_CPORTS="21,25,80,443,43"**—If you filter outgoing traffic, this is where you set what ports you want to allow out. Note that you should not put any cluster ports in here; you should allow only those ports for individual IP addresses for extra security, which we do later in this chapter, in the allow_hosts.rules file.

Finally, you should change the line right at the top of the file that by default is DEVM="1" and set it to DEVM="0". Otherwise, your firewall will disable itself every 5 minutes.

You should now configure the allow_hosts.rules file that sets out exceptions to the global rules listed in the main file for some IP addresses.

You have two choices with this file:

- You can allow all traffic, incoming and outgoing, for all IP addresses involved in your cluster.
- You can restrict access to only certain ports, even when the traffic originated and ended up in your cluster nodes.

This chapter covers how to do only the first option because it is perfectly secure and a lot easier and less likely to cause confusion. However, there is very good documentation for APF included with APF as well as excellent commenting of the allow_hosts.rules file, and if you want to lock everything down that little bit further, you can work out how to do it very quickly.

To allow all traffic from and to cluster nodes, in the file /etc/apf/allow_hosts.rules on all nodes, you simply put a list of the IP addresses of the nodes that make up your cluster, one per line. You then need to restart APF (by using service apf restart).

Standard Security Procedures

On any clean installation of MySQL, you should always ensure that MySQL is running as the unique and clearly defined underprivileged user mysql. This is the default behavior in most cases (in fact, it is quite difficult to run MySQL as root, but sometimes it can run as other users). To check your installation, you run the following command when MySQL is running:

```
[root@host]# ps aux | grep mysql
root      3749  0.0  0.4  5280 1060 ?        S    00:02   0:00 /bin/sh \
/usr/bin/mysqld_safe --pid-file=/var/run/mysqld/mysqld.pid
mysql     3778  0.0  1.1 124868 2820 ?       Sl   00:02   0:00 /usr/libexec/mysqld \
--defaults-file=/etc/my.cnf --basedir=/usr --datadir=/var/lib/mysql --user=mysql \
--pid-file=/var/run/mysqld/mysqld.pid --skip-locking \
--socket=/var/lib/mysql/mysql.sock
```

Notice that the /usr/libexec/mysqld daemon is running as the mysql user. If it is not (that is, if it is running as root), you need to follow these steps to make it run as a nonprivileged user:

1. Create the user mysql by using useradd mysql.

2. Stop the MySQL server by using service mysqld stop.

3. Change the ownership of DataDir (for both MySQL and MySQL Cluster), by using something like this:

```
chown -R mysql:mysql /var/lib/mysql
chown -R mysql:mysql /var/lib/mysql-cluster
```

4. Edit /etc/my.cnf to add user=mysql in the [mysqld] section.

5. Start MySQL server again by using service mysql start.

The other thing you should *always* do is to set a root password. This is so simple, yet many people fail to do it. After the installation process completes, you have a root user with no password. To change it, you run these commands:

```
[user@host]# mysql -u root
mysql> UPDATE mysql.user SET Password=PASSWORD('NEWPASSWORD')\
    ->WHERE User='root';
mysql> FLUSH PRIVILEGES;
```

If MySQL processes on your application servers are listening only on localhost, you can further increase security without using firewalls by adding skip-networking to the [mysqld] section of /etc/my.cnf to stop MySQL from responding to TCP/IP requests.

> **Note**
> You must ensure that all local scripts connect using a UNIX socket and not via a TCP/IP connection to 127.0.0.1. This can sometimes cause problems, although most of the time, anything that tries to connect to localhost will do so via a socket if possible because that is much more efficient.

> **An Important Note on Permissions Tables**
> All the tables in the mysql table (which contain all the information that MySQL requires, including the list of users and permissions) *must not* be converted to NDB format and must therefore not be clustered. MyISAM is an excellent format for these tables because they are likely to be read a lot and hardly ever written to. Converting them to any other storage engine is likely to result in instability, and converting them to NDB guarantees instability.
> If you have a large cluster and need to simplify management of it, you can use replication to maintain the mysql database (although you should make sure you set up replication *only* to replicate the mysql database—not the clustered databases, or you will get a mess). There are plans to allow the system tables to be switched into the NDB type in a future release of MySQL Cluster.

Managing MySQL Cluster

Managing a cluster in MySQL Cluster is likely to seem strange to you if you are used to installing a database server, configuring my.cnf, and forgetting about it (which many database administrators are). With MySQL Cluster, you need to proactively monitor your cluster to make sure that it remains healthy and well configured.

The following sections cover some tricks for managing a successful cluster.

The Management Console and Scripting

Appendix B, "Management Commands," provides a complete list of the commands you can use in the management console, and it is well worth experimenting with some of the less commonly used ones if you have the time.

To issue commands to the management console, you can either enter the console first and then issue the commands, as you have been doing so far, or you can issue them all on the command line with the -e flag, as in the following example:

```
[root@localhost mysql-cluster]# ndb_mgm -e SHOW
Connected to Management Server at: localhost:1186
Cluster Configuration
---------------------
[ndbd(NDB)]     2 node(s)
id=2    @192.168.254.21  (Version: 5.0.13, Nodegroup: 0, Master)
id=3    @192.168.254.22  (Version: 5.0.13, Nodegroup: 0)

[ndb_mgmd(MGM)] 1 node(s)
id=1    @192.168.254.20  (Version: 5.0.13)

[mysqld(API)]   2 node(s)
id=4    @192.168.254.21  (Version: 5.0.13)
id=5    @192.168.254.22  (Version: 5.0.13)
```

If you wanted to, you could put the following line in your crontab to email you the status of your cluster every day at 1 a.m.:

```
00 1 * * * /usr/bin/ndb_mgm -e show | \
mail -s "cluster status" youremail@yourdomain.tld
```

However, the trick of passing commands to ndb_mgm on the command line is more useful when it comes to running things regularly. For example, to run a backup every hour at half past the hour, you could enter the following line in your crontab:

```
30 * * * * /usr/bin/ndb_mgm -e "START BACKUP" \
| mail -s "backup results" youremail@yourdomain.tld
```

You could also write a simple script such as the following that emails you if any node disconnects for some reason:

```
#! /bin/bash
# check.sh - checks all cluster nodes connected
/usr/bin/ndb_mgm -e SHOW | grep -v grep | grep "not connected"  > /dev/null
if [ $? = 0 ]; then \
      /usr/bin/ndb_mgm -e SHOW | mail -s "CLUSTER ERROR: node down"
youremail@yourdomain.tld
fi ;
```

You will then get an email containing the following output if a node fails:

```
From: root <root@hostname>
To: youremail@yourdomain.tld
Subject: CLUSTER ERROR: node down

Connected to Management Server at: localhost:1186
Cluster Configuration
---------------------
[ndbd(NDB)]     2 node(s)
id=2 (not connected, accepting connect from 192.168.254.21)
id=3     @192.168.254.22  (Version: 5.0.13, Nodegroup: 0, Master)

[ndb_mgmd(MGM)]     1 node(s)
id=1     @192.168.254.20  (Version: 5.0.13)

[mysqld(API)]    2 node(s)
id=4     @192.168.254.21  (Version: 5.0.13)
id=5     @192.168.254.22  (Version: 5.0.13)
```

You can see that Node 2 has indeed died. You can run this script from cron every 5 minutes by putting the following line in crontab:

```
*/5 * * * * /root/scripts/check.sh >> /dev/null
```

As mentioned previously, however, this will fail if you have extra SQL nodes that are always not connected. The way to exclude these is to define their IDs and add a grep -v command to exclude them. For example, you might want to do this if you have the following cluster output when everything is working:

```
Cluster Configuration
---------------------
[ndbd(NDB)]     2 node(s)
id=2    @192.168.254.21  (Version: 5.0.13, Nodegroup: 0, Master)
id=3    @192.168.254.22  (Version: 5.0.13, Nodegroup: 0)

[ndb_mgmd(MGM)] 1 node(s)
id=1    @192.168.254.20  (Version: 5.0.13)

[mysqld(API)]   3 node(s)
id=4    @192.168.254.21  (Version: 5.0.13)
id=5    @192.168.254.22  (Version: 5.0.13)
id=6 (not connected, accepting connect from any host)
```

In other words, you want to exclude SQL node ID 6 from the alert system if it happens to be down. You can do this by using the following command:

```
/usr/bin/ndb_mgm -e SHOW | grep -v grep \
| grep -v id=6 | grep "not connected" > /dev/null
```

Doing a Rolling Cluster Restart

You will often find it useful to complete a rolling cluster restart—for example, after you have changed DataMemory or after you have upgraded your cluster nodes. The manual method for doing restarts is covered in Chapter 2, "Configuration." You have probably noticed that this is a time-consuming process that requires you to log in to each node. (Imagine how long this would take for clusters with more than 10 servers!) This section shows how to create a script that does this for you. This script needs to run on the management daemon, and it uses SSH between nodes; we strongly suggest that you set up authentication with keys to allow the management daemon to log in to the storage nodes as root without passwords. (Otherwise, you will have to enter the root password many times during the execution of the script.) You can find a guide to do this at this book's website, www.mysql-cluster.com.

Rather than just give the script to you in one piece, we have split it into sections and now explain what each does so you can modify it for your needs. Even if you are new to bash scripting, you should be able to make minor modifications to suit your particular needs.

> **Note**
> You can download a complete version of this script from www.mysql-cluster.com.

To start with, you define some variables for the whole script:

```
#! /bin/sh


#
# Restart all nodes with the --initial parameter
# Check each node comes back up before restarting next node
# Restart management daemon first.
#

# **NOTE**
# This script will only work if all storage nodes are
# currently "up" and working.


# Define variables

export CLUSTER_PATH="/var/lib/mysql-cluster"
#DataDir on the storage nodes

export NDB_MGMD="/usr/sbin/ndb_mgmd"
#Path to management daemon on management node (the node you run the script off)

export NDB_MGM="/usr/bin/ndb_mgm"
#Path to management client on management node

export NDBD="/usr/sbin/ndbd"
#Path to storage daemon on storage nodes

export RESTART_MYSQL="/etc/rc.d/init.d/mysql restart"
#Path to the mysql init script on the SQL nodes - on some distros this is
# different, e.g. /etc/init.d/mysqld restart

export STORAGE_NODES="192.168.254.21 192.168.254.22"
List of storage nodes (list of IP addresses separated by a space)

export SQL_NODES="192.168.254.21 192.168.254.22"
List of SQL nodes, as per list of storage nodes.
```

Now you have defined your variables, so this script must restart the management daemon. First, you check whether it is active, and if it is, you kill it. Then you start it, wait a few seconds, and check that it is still alive:

```
#
# PART 1: Restart Management Daemon
#
```

```
# Stop ndb_mgmd
ps -ef|grep ndb_mgmd|grep -v grep > /dev/null
if [ $? -eq 0 ]; then \
     echo "stopping ndb_mgmd on management node"
     pkill -9 ndb_mgmd
     echo "ndb_mgmd stopped"
     sleep 2;
fi ;

# Start ndb_mgmd
echo "starting ndb_mgmd from directory $CLUSTER_PATH";
cd $CLUSTER_PATH
$NDB_MGMD
echo -e "\nndb_mgmd started; checking that it is still alive in 2 seconds";
sleep 2;

# Check ndb_mgm is running
ps -ef | grep -v grep | grep ndb_mgmd  > /dev/null
if [ $? = 1 ]; then \
     # Means that ndb_mgmd was not found in process list
     echo "ndb_mgm is not running; aborting restart.";
     exit;
fi ;
echo "ndb_mgmd is still running; stage 1 success!";
```

Now the script needs to start restarting the storage nodes. It is critical that at any one time, it kills only one storage node so that the script will wait until each node hits the "started" state before moving on to the next node in the list. You *must* make sure that all storage nodes are started before you run this script; otherwise, you could potentially cause a cluster crash. Here is the next part of this script:

```
#
# PART 2: Restart Each storage node
#

for each in $STORAGE_NODES; do
     # Check if ndbd is running; stop it nicely if it is
     # and if it fails to stop kill it
     echo -e "\nChecking if ndbd is running on storage node $each"
     ssh -t $each 'ps -ef | grep -v grep | grep ndbd' > /dev/null
     if [ $? -eq 0 ]; then \
          echo "ndbd is already running on host $each; stopping process nicely"
          ndb_mgm -e "show" | grep -m 1 $each | awk '/id=/ { \
          print $1 }' | awk 'BEGIN { FS = "=" } ; { print $2 }';
          export NUM=`ndb_mgm -e "show" | grep -m 1 $each | \
          awk '/id=/ { print $1 }' | awk 'BEGIN { FS = "=" } ; { print $2 }'`
          ndb_mgm -e $NUM STOP
```

```
                sleep 10;
                echo "node given 10 seconds to die nicely, \
                now killing process just in case it is still alive"
                ssh -t $each pkill -9 ndbd
                echo "ndbd stopped on host $each"
                sleep 1;
        fi ;
        echo "Now starting ndbd on host $each"
        ssh -t $each $NDBD --initial
        echo "ndbd started on host $each"
        # Now, check that the node comes back up -
        # otherwise we risk a cluster crash if we repeat this loop
        # because we kill another node)

        echo -e "\nchecking that ndbd on host $each has completely started"
        echo "waiting for node on host $each to completely start"
        while true; do
            $NDB_MGM -e show | grep \
            "@$each  (Version: [[:digit:]][.][[:digit:]][.][[:digit:]][[:digit:]], \
            Nodegroup:" > /dev/null
            if [ $? = 1 ];
            then
                    echo "Waiting...."; sleep 3;
            else
                    echo "Node started OK"; sleep 5; break;
            fi
        done
done
```

As a final action, the script logs in to each SQL node to restart it. This is optional but often a good idea after a complete cluster restart:

```
#
# PART 3: Restart Each SQL node
#

for each in $SQL_NODES; do
        echo -e "\nRestarting SQL node $each"
        ssh -t $each $RESTART_MYSQL
done
```

To complete the process and for information only, the script now prints the new and completed status of the cluster:

```
echo -e "\n\nCluster status post-restart:"
$NDB_MGM -e show
```

```
for each in $SQL_NODES; do
      echo -e "\nRestarting SQL node $each"
      ssh -t $each $RESTART_MYSQL
done
```

Issuing a SQL Command to Each SQL Node

You will find that you often need to issue a SQL command to all your SQL nodes—for example, when adding a user (assuming that you have not set up replication for the mysql database) or when creating a database (which must be done on each SQL node before the node will "see" the database).

The following script will help you here. It logs you in from the local machine rather than logging in remotely, which allows it to log you in to nodes that only allow SQL access to the localhost. The only requirement is that the MySQL root password must be the same on each SQL node:

```
#! /bin/sh

#
# Issue SQL command to each SQL node in cluster
#

# Define variables

export ROOT_PASSWORD="mypass"
export DATABASE="mydb"
export SQL_QUERY="SELECT 1"
export SQL_NODES="192.168.254.21 192.168.254.22"

for each in $SQL_NODES; do
      echo -e "\nIssuing command to SQL node $each"
      ssh -t $each echo "$SQL_COMMAND" | /usr/bin/mysql \
      -uroot -p $ROOT_PASSWORD $DATABASE
done
```

Running MySQL in a Chrooted Environment

Chrooting is a verb created from the chroot(2) system call, which is a call made by processes that want to change the root of the file system they will see from then on.

When a process requests to chroot to a given directory, any future system calls issued by the process will see that directory as the file system root. It therefore becomes impossible for that process to access files and binaries outside the tree rooted on the new root directory. This environment is known as a chroot *jail*.

Running MySQL in a chrooted environment is another layer of security that starts with running your MySQL Cluster process as a different user (mysql). If you have MySQL running in a chrooted environment, you make it exceptionally difficult for a hacker to take the system down or take control of the system, even if the hacker manages to take control of the process via a vulnerability such as a buffer overflow.

It is *not* currently possible (as far as we can tell) to run the MySQL Cluster daemons in a chrooted environment, but you should run your SQL nodes in such an environment if at all possible. If you are trying to do this, it helps if you compile MySQL by using --with-mysqld-ldflags=-all-static to avoid having to put every library that MySQL Cluster requires in the chroot directory.

Getting MySQL to run in a chrooted enviroment is a very similar process to the process of compiling from source described in Chapter 1, "Installation," although there are subtle differences, and if you have already compiled from source, we recommend that you recompile. If you have already installed a MySQL binary, we recommend that you remove it by either deleting the folder if you downloaded a binary tarball or removing the RPMs.

To obtain the MySQL Cluster source, you use the following commands:

```
[root@host] cd /tmp/
[root@host] wget <url-of-mirror>/mysql-5.0.12-beta.tar.gz
[root@host] tar -zxvf mysql-5.0.12-beta.tar.gz
[root@host] cd  mysql-5.0.12-beta
```

Next, you compile and install it:

```
[root@host]  ./configure --prefix=/usr/local/mysql --with-ndbcluster \
>--with-mysqld-ldflags=-all-static --with-mysqld-user=mysql \
>--with-unix-socket-path=/tmp/mysql.sock
[root@host] make
[user@host] su -
[root@host] make test
[root@host] make install
[root@host] strip /usr/local/mysql/libexec/mysqld
[root@host] scripts/mysql_install_db
[root@host] cp support-files/my-medium.cnf /etc/my.cnf
```

Then you create the relevant directories in the chroot folder from which you want mysql to run:

```
[root@host] mkdir -p /chroot/mysql/dev /chroot/mysql/etc /chroot/mysql/tmp
[root@host] mkdir -p /chroot/mysql/var/tmp /chroot/mysql/usr/local/mysql/libexec
[root@host] mkdir -p /chroot/mysql/usr/local/mysql/share/mysql/english
```

Next, you set the correct directory permissions:

```
[root@host] chown -R root:sys /chroot/mysql
[root@host] chmod -R 755 /chroot/mysql
[root@host] chmod 1777 /chroot/mysql/tmp
```

When the directories are set up, you copy the server's files:

```
[root@host] cp /usr/local/mysql/libexec/mysqld \
>/chroot/mysql/usr/local/mysql/libexec/
[root@host] cp /usr/local/mysql/share/mysql/english/errmsg.sys \
>/chroot/mysql/usr/local/mysql/share/mysql/english/
[root@host] cp -r /usr/local/mysql/share/mysql/charsets \
>/chroot/mysql/usr/local/mysql/share/mysql/
[root@host] cp /etc/hosts /chroot/mysql/etc/
[root@host] cp /etc/host.conf /chroot/mysql/etc/
[root@host] cp /etc/resolv.conf /chroot/mysql/etc/
[root@host] cp /etc/group /chroot/mysql/etc/
[root@host] cp /etc/my.cnf /chroot/mysql/etc/
```

Then you copy the mysql databases that contain the grant tables (created by mysql_install_db) that store the MySQL access privileges:

```
[root@host] cp -R /usr/local/mysql/var/ /chroot/mysql/usr/local/mysql/var
[root@host] chown -R mysql:mysql /chroot/mysql/usr/local/mysql/var
```

Next, you create a null device within the chroot:

```
[root@host] mknod /chroot/mysql/dev/null c 2 2
[root@host] chown root:sys /chroot/mysql/dev/null
[root@host] chmod 666 /chroot/mysql/dev/null
```

You then need to edit a few files to remove all users and groups apart from mysql in the chroot environment (this prevents any other user from running inside the chroot jail and is critical for the security of the jail).

In the file /chroot/mysql/etc/group, you delete all lines except the following:

```
root:x:0:
mysql:x:500:
```

In file /chroot/mysql/etc/passwords, delete all lines apart from

```
root:x:0:0:MySQL Cluster:/dev/null:/bin/false
mysql:x:500:501:MySQL Server:/dev/null:/bin/false
```

In order to run MySQL as a nonprivileged user, you need to install the chrootuid package:

```
[root@host] cd /usr/src/
[root@host] wget ftp://ftp.porcupine.org/pub/security/chrootuid1.3.tar.gz
[root@host] tar -zxvf chrootuid1.3.tar.gz
```

```
[root@host] cd chrootuid1.3
[root@host] make
[root@host] make install
```

Now, if you have done all this correctly, you can start mysql by using the following command:

```
[root@host] chrootuid /chroot/mysql mysql /usr/local/mysql/libexec/mysqld &
```

Finally, you need to create a symlink from /tmp/mysql.sock to the chroot /tmp/mysql.sock so you can connect to your server locally:

```
[root@host] ln -s /chroot/mysql/tmp/mysql.sock /tmp/mysql.sock
```

You should now be able to start the mysql client:

```
[root@host] mysql
Welcome to the MySQL monitor.  Commands end with ; or \g.
Your MySQL connection id is 2 to server version: 5.0.12-beta-log

Type 'help;' or '\h' for help. Type '\c' to clear the buffer.

mysql> show databases;
+--------------------+
| Database           |
+--------------------+
| information_schema |
| mysql              |
| test               |
+--------------------+
3 rows in set (0.03 sec)

mysql>
```

Your application should now be able to connect to the chrooted MySQL process, which should still work fine when it comes to connecting to the other nodes in the cluster.

If you consider security as a process of putting up walls for attackers, you should continue to put up walls until such a time as the cost to you (either in terms of time, money, or hassle for your users) becomes greater than the return that the extra wall gives you in terms of extra security. Few users actually run MySQL in a chrooted environment unless they are in a high-risk environment (for example, shared hosting), but it is an option worth considering.

Performance

Performance is a very important topic when dealing with any database setup. One of the main reasons to use a cluster over a nonclustered database is the ability to get better performance and scalability compared to using a database that is confined to a single host. This chapter discusses many of the concepts related to performance and scalability, as well as how to ensure that you get the maximum from your MySQL Cluster setup.

Performance Metrics

Before we get into performance tuning, we need to discuss what performance means, as it can have different meanings to different people. Many different metrics can go into measuring performance and scalability, but the overall definition we use in this book is "ensuring that every client's needs are satisfied as quickly as possible." Beyond this definition, we can talk about many other related topics as well, such as response time, throughput, and scalability.

Response time indicates how long someone has to wait to be served. There are some different metrics based on this that are worth monitoring. First is maximum response time, which indicates how long anyone has to wait in the worst-case scenario. The second is the average response time, which is useful for knowing what the average response time is. Keep in mind that response time normally includes two different pieces of the time for a response: wait time and execution time. Wait time, or queue time, is how long the client has to block (that is, wait in a queue for access) before execution can begin. This wait occurs normally due to lock contention. Execution time is the amount of time actually spent running (that is, executing) statements.

Throughput is a metric that measures how many clients and requests you serve over some time period. Typically you might see this measured as queries per second or transactions per minute.

Finally, *scalability* is how well the previous two values can be maintained as the overall load increases. This increase in load might be tied to the number of database users, or it could possibly be independent of that. Sometimes, multiple dimensions of load increase at the same time. For example, as the number of users increases, the amount of data and the number of queries may both increase. This is often one of the hardest pieces to be sure of, due to the fact that it can be difficult to simulate the exact effects of these increases without them actually occurring.

MySQL Cluster Performance

MySQL Cluster has a very different impact on the concepts of response time, throughput, and scalability than a normal single-system, disk-based database, such as MyISAM or InnoDB.

Response time with MySQL Cluster is quite commonly worse than it is with the traditional setup. Yes, response time is quite commonly worse with clustering than with a normal system. If you consider the architecture of MySQL Cluster, this will begin to make more sense. When you do a query with a cluster, it has to first go to the MySQL server, and then it goes to data nodes and sends the data back the same way. When you do a query on a normal system, all access is done within the MySQL server itself. It is clearly faster to access local resources than to read the same thing across a network. As discussed later in this chapter, response time is very much dependant on network latency because of the extra network traffic. Some queries may be faster than others due to the parallel scanning that is possible, but you cannot expect all queries to have a better response time. So if the response time is worse, why would you use a cluster? First, response time isn't normally very important. For the vast majority of applications, 10ms versus 15ms isn't considered a big difference. Where MySQL Cluster shines is in relation to the other two metrics—throughput and scalability.

Throughput and scalability are generally much better with clustering than in a single-system database. If you consider the most common bottlenecks of the different systems, you can see why. With a single-system database, you almost always bottleneck on disk I/O. As you get more users and queries, disk I/O generally becomes slower due to extra seeking overhead. For example, if you are doing 1Mbps worth of access with one client, you might only be able to do 1.5Mbps with two and only 1.75Mbps with three clients. MySQL Cluster is typically bottlenecked on network I/O. Network traffic scales much better with multiple users. For example, if you are transferring 1Mbps with one client, you can do 2Mbps with two clients, 3Mbps with three clients, and so on. You start to have problems only when you near the maximum possible throughput. This allows you to scale the system relatively easily until you start to reach network limits, which are generally are quite high.

Benchmarking

Benchmarking is a tool that, when used correctly, can help you plan for scalability, test throughput, and measure response time. When used incorrectly, benchmarking can give you a very wrong impression of these things.

In a good benchmark, you want to simulate your production environment as closely as possible. This includes things such as hardware available, software being used, and usage patterns.

The following sections describe some common problems with benchmarks.

Using the Wrong Data Size

When doing a benchmark, you need to have the same amount of data you plan on having in the system. Doing a benchmark with 50MB of data when you plan on having 10GB in production is not a useful benchmark.

Using a Data Set That Is Not Representative

If you are generating data, you need to make sure it isn't too random. In real life, most data has patterns that cause more repeats of certain data than of other data. For example, imagine that you have a set of categories for something. In real life, certain categories are likely to be much more common than other categories. If you have exactly the same distribution of these in your generated data, this can influence the benchmark.

Using Inaccurate Data Access Patterns

Using inaccurate data access patterns is similar to using a data set that is not representative, but it relates to data access instead. For example, if in your benchmark you are searching for "Latin dictionary" as commonly as "Harry Potter," you will see different effects. Some things are much more commonly accessed than others, and your benchmarks need to take that into account.

Failing to Consider Cache Effects

There are two ways failing to consider cache effects can affect your benchmarking. First, you can run a benchmark that makes overly heavy use of caches. For example, if you run just the same query over and over, caching plays a very big role in it. Second, you can do completely different things over and over, which reduces the effectiveness of caches. This relates to the previously mentioned concept of data access patterns. "Harry Potter" would most likely have a high cache hit rate, but "Latin dictionary" wouldn't make as much use of the cache, and this can be difficult to measure in benchmarks.

Using Too Little Load or Too Few Users

In order for a benchmark to be accurate, it needs to reflect the number of users who will be accessing your system. A very common problem with MySQL Cluster benchmarks is attempting to benchmark with only a single user (which MySQL Cluster is quite poor at due to bad response time, but it has great scalability and throughput).

Benchmarking Solutions

Now that you know some of the problems with benchmarking, how can you work around them? One of the easiest ways is to benchmark against your actual application. For some application types, such as web applications, this is very easy to do. Two commonly used web benchmarking applications that are available for free are httperf (www.hpl.hp.com/research/linux/httperf/) and Microsoft Web Application Stress Tool (www.microsoft.com/technet/archive/itsolutions/intranet/downloads/webstres.mspx). For some application types, such as embedded applications, benchmarking is more difficult, and you may need to create a tool yourself.

The other solution is to use a benchmarking tool that can more closely mimic your application. Two tools in this category are Super Smack (http://vegan.net/tony/supersmack/) and mybench (http://jeremy.zawodny.com/mysql/mybench/). With both of these tools, you can more accurately represent what the query/user/data patterns are for your application. They require quite a bit of customization, but they can help you avoid some of the common pitfalls.

Indexes

Indexes are extremely important in MySQL Cluster, just as they are with other database engines. MySQL Cluster has three different types of indexes: PRIMARY KEY indexes, UNIQUE hash indexes, and ordered indexes (T-tree).

PRIMARY KEY Indexes

The data in MySQL Cluster is partitioned based on a hash of the PRIMARY KEY column(s). This means the primary key is implemented through a hash index type. A hash index can be used to resolve queries that are used with equals but cannot be used for range scans. In addition, you need to use all of a PRIMARY KEY column and not just part of it.

The following is an example of queries that could use the PRIMARY KEY column:

```
SELECT * FROM tbl WHERE pk = 5;
SELECT * FROM tbl WHERE pk = 'ABC' OR pk = 'XYZ';
```

The following are examples of queries that will not use the PRIMARY KEY index:

```
SELECT * FROM tbl WHERE pk < 100;
SELECT * FROM tbl WHERE pk_part1 = 'ABC';
```

The first of these examples will not use the PRIMARY KEY index because it involves a range with less than and not a straight equality. The second example assumes that you have a two-part primary key, such as PRIMARY KEY (pk_part1, pk_part2). Because the query is using only the first half, it cannot be used.

Using the primary key is the fastest way to access a single row in MySQL due to the fact that your tables are partitioned on it.

Remember that when you declare a primary key in MySQL Cluster, by default you get both the PRIMARY KEY hash index and an ordered index, as described in the following section. It is possible to force the primary key to have only a hash index if you aren't going to be doing range lookups. Here is how you implement that:

```
PRIMARY KEY (col) USING HASH
```

UNIQUE Hash Indexes

UNIQUE hash indexes occur whenever you declare a UNIQUE constraint in MySQL Cluster. They are implemented through a secondary table that has the column you declared UNIQUE as the primary key in the table along with the primary key of the base table:

```
CREATE TABLE tbl (
        Id int auto_increment,
        Name char(50),
        PRIMARY KEY (id),
        UNIQUE (Name)
);
```

This gives you a hidden table that looks like the following:

```
CREATE TABLE hidden (
        Name_hash char(8),
        Orig_pk int,
        PRIMARY KEY (name_hash)
);
```

These tables are independently partitioned, so the index may not reside on the same node as the data does. This causes UNIQUE indexes to be slightly slower than the PRIMARY KEY, but they will still be extremely fast for most lookups.

Ordered Indexes

An ordered index in MySQL Cluster is implemented through a structure called a T-tree. A T-tree works the same as a B-tree, but it is designed for use with in-memory databases. The two primary differences are that a T-tree is generally much deeper than a B-tree (because it doesn't have to worry about disk seek times) and that a T-tree doesn't contain the actual data itself, but just a pointer to the data, which makes a T-tree take up less memory than a similar B-tree.

All the queries that could be resolved with a B-tree index can also be resolved by using a T-tree index. This includes all the normal range scans, such as less than, between, and greater than. So if you are switching an application from MyISAM or InnoDB to MySQL Cluster, it should continue to work the same for query plans.

A T-tree itself is partitioned across the data nodes. Each data node contains a part of the T-tree that corresponds to the data that it has locally.

Index Statistics

The MySQL optimizer uses various statistics in order to decide which is the most optimal method for resolving a query. MySQL particularly makes use of two different values: the number of rows in the table and an estimate of how many rows will match a particular condition.

The first value is approximately the number of rows in a table. This is important for deciding whether MySQL should do a full table scan or use indexes. MySQL Cluster can provide this value to the MySQL optimizer, but it doesn't necessarily have to do so. The problem with retrieving this data from the data nodes for each query being executed is that it adds a bit of extra overhead and slightly degrades the response time of your queries. There is therefore a way to turn off the fetching of the exact number of rows. The MySQL server setting ndb_use_exact_count controls whether to do the retrieval. If the MySQL server doesn't retrieve an exact value, it will always say there are 100 rows in the table.

Due to the distributed and in-memory natures of the MySQL storage engine, it is almost always best to use an index, if possible. In most cases, you want to turn off the ndb_use_exact_count variable to gain performance because it favors index reads.

As a side note, the ndb_use_exact_count variable has an impact on the following simple statement:

```
SELECT count(*) FROM tbl;
```

If you are familiar with the other storage engines, you know that MyISAM has an optimization to speed this up, whereas InnoDB doesn't. The ndb_use_exact_count setting affects NDB in a similar manner: If it is on, it works like MyISAM, but if it is off, it works like InnoDB. The nice thing is that you can set this on a per-connection basis, which allows you to do something such as the following:

```
mysql> set ndb_use_exact_count = 1;
Query OK, 0 rows affected (0.00 sec)

root@world~> SELECT count(*) FROM Country;
+----------+
| count(*) |
+----------+
|      239 |
+----------+
1 row in set (0.01 sec)

mysql> set ndb_use_exact_count = 0;
Query OK, 0 rows affected (0.01 sec)
```

The other value that MySQL uses is an estimation of how many rows will match against a particular index lookup. MySQL Cluster currently isn't able to calculate this value. It always estimates that 10 rows will match. If you combine this with the preceding rule of 100 rows, you see that MySQL will always use indexes, which is good with MySQL Cluster. Where the problem comes with this is where MySQL has choices between multiple indexes. The following query shows the problem:

```
SELECT * FROM tbl WHERE idx1 = 5 AND idx2 = 10;
```

MySQL Cluster tells MySQL that both idx1 and idx2 will retrieve the same number of rows (10). However, normally this might not be true; one of the indexes is typically more selective than the other. In this case, because MySQL Cluster doesn't have the information available, you have to tell MySQL which one is better. To tell it which one, you should use a USING INDEX clause in the SELECT statement. So if the second index is more selective, you write a statement similar to the following:

```
SELECT * FROM tbl USING INDEX (idx2) WHERE idx1 = 5 AND idx2 = 10;
```

MySQL 5.1 will have the ability for NDB to estimate the rows that will match when using an index. This will prevent you from having to tell MySQL which index is more selective in most cases.

Query Execution

Query execution in MySQL Cluster can use a couple different methods. Which method is used makes a large difference in the response time of a query.

When MySQL receives a query, many different steps occur before you receive the results. The path is roughly laid out like this:

1. Receive query over network
2. Check query cache
3. Parse query
4. Check permissions
5. Optimize query:
   a. Query transformations
   b. Decide the order in which to read the tables
   c. Decide on index use
   d. Decide which algorithms to use for retrieval

6. Query execution:
   a. Retrieval of data, based on preceding plan
   b. Apply expressions to retrieved data
   c. Sort data as necessary

7. Return results back to client

MySQL Cluster comes into play in step 5(a). MySQL Cluster is the storage engine that does the actual physical retrieval of data. All the other steps are done on the MySQL server side and work the same as with other storage engines. Before we talk further about this, we need to discuss the one other step that is affected as well: the query cache.

The Query Cache in MySQL Cluster

The query cache is a special cache that exists in MySQL to cache a query and a result set. If someone sends exactly the same query again, MySQL can return the result set directly from the cache instead of having to execute it again. When the data in a table changes, the query cache invalidates all the queries that involve that table, in order to prevent serving stale data. This is generally how it works with MySQL, but it gets a bit more involved with MySQL Cluster.

First, the query cache doesn't work at all with MySQL Cluster version 4.1. This shortcoming has been fixed in MySQL 5.0, but it does work slightly differently. The reason it works differently is that data can change in many different MySQL servers without the other MySQL servers being aware of the changes. If the server isn't aware of changes, then it can't invalidate the cache, which leads to incorrect results.

When you have the query cache on and NDB enabled, MySQL creates an extra thread internally to periodically check what tables have been changed. Doing this check causes a bit of extra overhead for the MySQL server. Due to this extra overhead, you need to keep a few things in mind.

First, you should ensure that you are getting good use of the query cache. You can monitor the query cache status variables in order to see what percentage of them are using the cache:

```
mysql> SHOW STATUS LIKE 'Qcache%';
+-------------------------+----------+
| Variable_name           | Value    |
+-------------------------+----------+
| Qcache_free_blocks      | 1        |
| Qcache_free_memory      | 10476984 |
| Qcache_hits             | 32342    |
| Qcache_inserts          | 2323     |
| Qcache_lowmem_prunes    | 2        |
| Qcache_not_cached       | 20       |
| Qcache_queries_in_cache | 32       |
| Qcache_total_blocks     | 36       |
+-------------------------+----------+
8 rows in set (0.00 sec)
```

The important variables to monitor are Qcache_hits, Qcache_inserts, and Qcache_not_cached. You need to ensure that Qcache_hits is generally larger than the other two values added together (which is the query cache miss rate).

The second thing you can do is change a value called `ndb_check_cache_time`. This variable tells how many seconds MySQL Cluster should wait between checking for data changes that were made on another MySQL server. The default setting is 0, which means MySQL Cluster will constantly be checking. Increasing this variable greatly reduces the overhead, but, in theory, it means there is a chance that the query cache will return slightly incorrect data. For example, it might return incorrect data if someone changes data on one server and any queries until the next server checks for that change return incorrect data. Whether this is okay depends entirely on the application. Normally any setting above 1 wouldn't be needed because the server checks only once per second for invalidations.

Data Retrieval in MySQL Cluster

MySQL Cluster has four different methods of retrieving data with different performance characteristics: primary key access, unique key access, ordered index access, and full table scans.

Primary Key Access

When a query is going to use the primary key, it does so using a normal hash lookup. The MySQL server forms a hash of the primary key, and then, using the same algorithm for partitioning, it knows exactly which data node contains the data and fetches it from there, as shown in Figure 5.1. This process is identical, no matter how many data nodes are present.

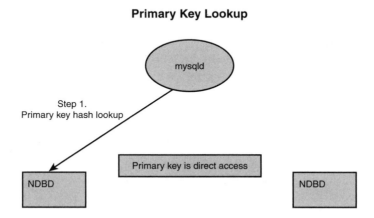

FIGURE 5.1   Primary key access.

Unique Key Access

When a query is going to use a unique key, it again does a hash lookup. However, in this case, it is a two-step process, as shown in Figure 5.2. The query first uses a hash on the

UNIQUE value to look up the PRIMARY KEY value that corresponds to the row. It does this by using the value as the primary key into the hidden table. Then, when it has the primary key from the base table, it is able to retrieve the data from the appropriate place. For response time purposes, a UNIQUE access is approximately double the response time of a primary key lookup because it has to do two primary key lookups to get the row.

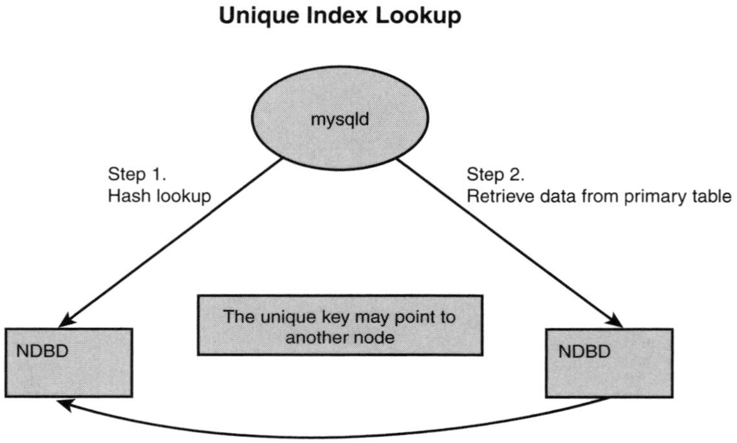

Unique Index Lookup

FIGURE 5.2   Unique key access.

Ordered Index Access

To access an ordered index, the MySQL server does what is a called a *parallel index scan*, as shown in Figure 5.3. Essentially, this means that it has to ask every single data node to look through the piece of the index that the data node has locally. The nodes do this in parallel, and the MySQL server combines the results as they are returned to the server from the data nodes.

Due to the parallel nature of the scanning, this can, in theory, have a better response time than doing a local query. This is not always true, however, as it depends on many different things.

An ordered index scan causes more network traffic and is more expensive than a PRIMARY KEY or UNIQUE KEY lookup. However, it can resolve a lot of queries that cannot be resolved by using a hash lookup.

Full Table Scan

The final method for resolving a query is through the use of a full table scan. MySQL Cluster can do this in two different ways, depending on the version and startup options you use for the MySQL server:

- **Full table scan without condition pushdown**—This first option is the slower, less efficient method. In this method, all the data in the table is fetched back to the MySQL server, which then applies a WHERE clause to the data. As you can imagine, this is a very expensive operation. If you have a table that is 2GB in size, this operation results in all 2GB of data crossing the network every time you do a full table scan. This method is the only one available in MySQL 4.1. It is also the default method in MySQL 5.0.

- **Full table scan with condition pushdown**—There is an option in MySQL 5.0 called engine_condition_pushdown. If this option is turned on, the MySQL server can attempt to do a more optimized method for the full table scan. In this case, the WHERE clause that you are using to filter the data is sent to each of the data nodes. Each of the data nodes can then apply the condition before it sends the data back across the network. This generally reduces the amount of data being returned and can speed up the query over the previous method by a great deal. Imagine that you have a table with 2 million rows, but you are retrieving only 10 rows, based on the WHERE condition. With the old method, you would send 2 million rows across the network; with the new method, you would only have to send the 10 rows that match across the network. This reduces the network traffic by almost 99.9999%. As you can imagine, this is normally the preferred method.

Parallel Scans

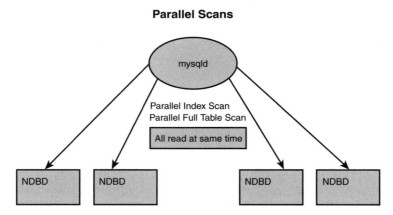

FIGURE 5.3   Ordered index access.

To enable the engine_condition_pushdown option, you need to set it in the MySQL configuration file:

```
[mysqld]
ndbcluster
engine_condition_pushdown=1
```

You can also set it dynamically by using either the SET GLOBAL or SET SESSION command, like this:

```
SET SESSION engine_condition_pushdown=1;
SET GLOBAL engine_condition_pushdown=0;
```

SET GLOBAL applies to all future connections. SET SESSION applies to only the current connection. Keep in mind that if you want to have the value survive across a MySQL server, you should restart and then change the configuration file.

You can verify that the engine_condition_pushdown variable is currently on by using the SHOW VARIABLES command:

```
mysql> show variables like 'engine%';
+--------------------------+-------+
| Variable_name            | Value |
+--------------------------+-------+
| engine_condition_pushdown | ON   |
+--------------------------+-------+
1 row in set (0.00 sec)
```

After this variable has been set, you can ensure that it is actually working by using the EXPLAIN command. If it is working, you see the Extra option called "Using where with pushed condition":

```
mysql> EXPLAIN SELECT * FROM country WHERE name LIKE '%a%'\G
*************************** 1. row ***************************
           id: 1
  select_type: SIMPLE
        table: country
         type: ALL
possible_keys: NULL
          key: NULL
      key_len: NULL
          ref: NULL
         rows: 239
        Extra: Using where with pushed condition
1 row in set (0.00 sec)
```

Using EXPLAIN

The EXPLAIN command is the key to knowing which of the access methods are being used and how MySQL is resolving your query.

To use EXPLAIN, all you have to do is prefix your SELECT statement with the keyword EXPLAIN, as in the following example:

> **Note**
>
> Note that these examples use the world database, which is freely available from the documentation section of http://dev.mysql.com.
>
> If you want to try out these exact examples, you can download and install the world database and switch all the tables to NDB by using ALTER TABLE. Remember to create the database world on all SQL nodes.

```
mysql> EXPLAIN SELECT * FROM Country, City WHERE Country.capital = City.id
    AND Country.region LIKE 'Nordic%'\G
*************************** 1. row ***************************
           id: 1
  select_type: SIMPLE
        table: Country
         type: ALL
possible_keys: NULL
          key: NULL
      key_len: NULL
          ref: NULL
         rows: 239
        Extra: Using where
*************************** 2. row ***************************
           id: 1
  select_type: SIMPLE
        table: City
         type: eq_ref
possible_keys: PRIMARY
          key: PRIMARY
      key_len: 4
          ref: world.Country.Capital
         rows: 1
        Extra:
2 rows in set (0.00 sec)
```

There is a lot of information here, so let's examine what it all means.

The first significant thing we need to examine is the order in which the rows come back. The order is the order in which MySQL is going to read the tables. This order does not normally depend on the order in which they are listed in the query. For inner joins and some outer joins, MySQL rearranges the tables into any order it feels will make your query faster.

The next thing that is important is the Type column. It tells how MySQL is going to read the table. This ties in to the previous section about table access methods. Some of the possible retrieval types and what they correspond to for MySQL Cluster are listed in Table 5.1.

TABLE 5.1   **Retrieval Types in MySQL Cluster**

EXPLAIN type	Cluster Access Method	Description
Const	Primary key, unique key	MySQL knows there is at most one matching row. MySQL can read that row and optimize the table from the query. This is a very good access method.
eq_ref	Primary key, unique key	This is a join on a unique column. It is a very fast join method.
Ref	Ordered index	This is a scan using a non-unique index.
Range	Ordered index	This is a retrieve range of data based on non-equality (that is, less than, BETWEEN, LIKE).
ALL	Full table scan	MySQL will read the entire table.

The next two columns in EXPLAIN are possible_keys and key. These columns indicate which indexes MySQL is using and also which indexes it sees are possible but decides not to use to resolve your query. Due to the lack of index statistics, as mentioned previously in this chapter, you might consider suggesting one of the other possible indexes with USE INDEX to see if it is any faster with a different one.

The next column of significance is the rows column. This column tells how many rows MySQL thinks it will have to read from the table for each previous combination of rows. However, this number generally isn't all that accurate because NDB does not give accurate statistics to MySQL. Normally, if you are using an index, you will see 10 listed as the rows, regardless of how many rows actually match. If you are doing a full table scan, you will also see 100 if ndb_use_exact_count is turned off. If ndb_use_exact_count is enabled, the rows column correctly gives the number of rows in the table that need to be scanned.

The final column listed is the Extra column. This column can list any additional information about how the query is going to be executed. The first important value that can show up here is Using where with pushed condition. As mentioned previously, this means that NDB is able to send out the WHERE condition to the data nodes in order to filter data for a full table scan. A similar possible value is Using where. This value indicates that the MySQL server isn't able to send the filtering condition out to the data nodes. If you see this, you can attempt to get the MySQL server to send it out in order to possibly speed up the query.

The first thing you can do is ensure that the engine_condition_pushdown variable is set. You can view whether it is set by using the SHOW VARIABLES option:

```
mysql> EXPLAIN SELECT * FROM Country WHERE code LIKE '%a%'\G
*************************** 1. row ***************************
          id: 1
 select_type: SIMPLE
       table: Country
        type: ALL
```

```
possible_keys: NULL
          key: NULL
      key_len: NULL
          ref: NULL
         rows: 239
        Extra: Using where
1 row in set (0.14 sec)

mysql> show variables like 'engine_condition_pushdown';
+--------------------------+-------+
| Variable_name            | Value |
+--------------------------+-------+
| engine_condition_pushdown | OFF   |
+--------------------------+-------+
1 row in set (0.01 sec)

root@world~> set session engine_condition_pushdown=1;
Query OK, 0 rows affected (0.00 sec)

mysql> explain SELECT * FROM Country WHERE code LIKE '%a%'\G
*************************** 1. row ***************************
           id: 1
  select_type: SIMPLE
        table: Country
         type: ALL
possible_keys: NULL
          key: NULL
      key_len: NULL
          ref: NULL
         rows: 239
        Extra: Using where with pushed condition
1 row in set (0.00 sec)
```

The second method you can attempt is to rewrite the query into something that can be pushed down. In order to be able to push down a WHERE condition, it has to follow these rules:

- Any columns used must not be used in expressions (that is, no calculations or functions on them).
- The comparison must be one of the supported types. Supported types include the following:
  - =, !=, >, >=, <, <=, IS NULL, and IS NOT NULL
  - Combinations of the preceding types (for example, BETWEEN, IN())
- AND and OR are allowed.

The following is an example of how to rewrite a query to make use of the condition pushdown:

```
mysql> explain SELECT * FROM Country WHERE population/1.2 < 1000
    OR code LIKE '%a%' \G
*************************** 1. row ***************************
          id: 1
 select_type: SIMPLE
       table: Country
        type: ALL
possible_keys: NULL
         key: NULL
     key_len: NULL
         ref: NULL
        rows: 239
       Extra: Using where
1 row in set (0.09 sec)

mysql> explain SELECT * FROM Country WHERE population < 1000/1.2
    OR code LIKE '%a%' \G
*************************** 1. row ***************************
          id: 1
 select_type: SIMPLE
       table: Country
        type: ALL
possible_keys: NULL
         key: NULL
     key_len: NULL
         ref: NULL
        rows: 239
       Extra: Using where with pushed condition
1 row in set (0.00 sec)
```

Notice that in the second `explain`, the query was rewritten to put the `population` column used all by itself on one side. That allowed the condition to be pushed down, which will potentially enable the full table scan to be many times faster.

Physical Factors

One of the most important factors when dealing with the response time of MySQL Cluster is network latency. The lower the network latency, the lower the response time.

Any operation that occurs within MySQL Cluster normally has numerous round trips across the network as messages are passed around between data nodes and the MySQL server. For example, during a transaction commit, NDB needs to do a two-phase commit procedure, which ensures that all the data nodes have the correct data (due to synchronous replication).

The number of operations performed during a two-phase commit is measured as follows:

Num. of Messages = 2 × Num. of Fragments × (NoOfReplicas + 1)

Assume that you have four data nodes with NoOfReplicas set to 2. That gives us $2 \times 4 \times (2 + 1) = 24$ messages. If we have a latency of .5ms between nodes, that gives us a total network time of $24 \times .5 = 12$ms. Reducing the latency by even a little bit will make a relatively large difference due the number of messages.

There are a few things to note with this. First, most operations do not involve so many messages. For example, a single primary key lookup results in just two messages: the request for the row and the return of the row. Network latency still plays a big part in response time, but the effects of changing the latency are smaller for some messages due to the smaller number of messages.

The second important concept to mention is message grouping. Because so many messages are being passed by MySQL Cluster in a highly concurrent environment, MySQL can attempt to piggyback messages on other ones. For example, if two people are reading data at the same time, even from different tables, the messages can be combined into a single network packet. Because of the way network communications work, this can improve throughput and allow for much more concurrency before the network becomes saturated by lowering the overhead for each message. The drawback of this grouping is that there is a slight delay before requests are sent. This slight delay causes a decrease in response time. In many cases, this is totally acceptable for the increase in throughput.

In some cases, the extra delay introduced by this isn't useful. The two most common cases are when there isn't a lot of concurrency and when response time is more important than throughput. In a situation of low concurrency, such as initial data imports, benchmarks that are being done with only a single thread, or little-used applications (for example, five queries per second), it makes sense to disable this optimization. The variable ndb_force_send can control this behavior. If this variable is turned off, MySQL Cluster groups together messages, if possible, introducing a slight response time decrease. If it is turned on, it attempts to group messages together, which should increase throughput.

High-Speed Interconnects

In order to get the best response time and to increase throughput, the most important physical aspect is the network interconnect.

NDB currently supports three different connection methods, also called *transports*: TCP/IP, shared memory, and SCI. It is possible to mix different transports within the same cluster, but it is recommended that all the data nodes use the same transport among themselves, if possible. The default if you don't specify is to use TCP/IP for all the nodes.

TCP/IP

TCP/IP is by far the most common connection protocol used in NDB. This is due to the fact that it is the default and also is normally preconfigured on most servers. The management node always makes use of TCP/IP. It cannot use shared memory or SCI. Normally, the fact that it can't use a high-speed interconnect should not be an issue because there isn't very much data being transferred between the management node and others.

TCP/IP is available over many different mediums. For a base cluster in MySQL Cluster, Gigabit Ethernet would be the minimum recommended connection. It is possible to run a cluster on less than that, such as a 100MB network, but doing so definitely affects performance.

Generally, you want your networking hardware to be high quality. It is possible to get network cards that can do much of the TCP/IP implementation. This helps to offload CPU usage from your nodes, but it will generally lower network latency slightly. Each little bit that you can save on network latency helps.

If you are looking for even higher performance over TCP/IP, it is possible to use some even higher network or clustering interconnects. For example, there is now 10GB Ethernet, which may increase performance over Gigabit Ethernet. There are also special clustering interconnects, such as Myrinet, that can make use of the TCP/IP transport as well. Myrinet is a commonly used network transport in clusters. Because it can use TCP/IP, it can be used with MySQL Cluster as well.

When examining the more expensive options, we highly recommend that you acquire test hardware if possible. Many of these interconnects cost many times what commodity hardware, such as Gigabit Ethernet, costs. In some applications, interconnects can make a large performance difference, but in others, they may not make a very great difference. If the performance isn't much better, it might be wiser to spend more of your budget on something else, such as more nodes.

Shared Memory

MySQL Cluster can make use of shared memory connections. Shared memory connections are also referred to as the SHM transport. This type of connection works only when two nodes reside on the same physical machine. Most commonly, this is between a MySQL server and a data node that reside locally, but it can be used between data nodes as well.

Generally, shared memory connections are faster than TCP/IP local connections. Shared memory connections require more CPU, however, so they are not always faster due to CPU bottlenecks. Whether a CPU bottleneck decreases performance is highly application specific. We recommend that you do some benchmark testing between shared memory and TCP/IP local connections to see which is better for your particular application.

In order to use the NDB shared memory transport, you need to ensure that the version you are using has the transport compiled in. Unfortunately, not all the operating systems that support MySQL Cluster contain the necessary pieces to support shared memory connections. If you are compiling yourself, you need to compile MySQL with the option `--with-ndb-shm`.

When you are sure that your platform contains the transport, you need to configure MySQL Cluster to use it. There are two different ways to configure shared memory connections. The first option is designed to allow for more automatic configuration of shared memory. The second requires manual configuration but is a bit more flexible.

The first option is controlled by a startup option for the MySQL server called `ndb-shm`. When you start `mysqld` with this option, it causes `mysqld` to automatically attempt to use shared memory for connections, if possible. Obviously, this works only when connecting to local data nodes, but you can run with this option regardless of whether there are any local data nodes.

The second option is to set up shared memory by putting it in the cluster configuration file (normally `config.ini`). For each shared memory connection you want, you need to add a `[SHM]` group. The required settings are the two node IDs involved and a unique integer identifier. Here is an example:

```
[SHM]
NodeId1=3
NodeId2=4
ShmKey=324
```

`NodeId1` and `NodeId2` refer to the two nodes you want to communicate over shared memory. You need a separate `[SHM]` section for each set of two nodes. For example, if you have three local data nodes, you need to define three `[SHM]` sections (that is, 1–2, 2–3, and 1–3).

You may want to define some optional settings as well. The most common setting is called `ShmSize`. It designates the size of the shared memory segment to use for communication. The default is 1MB, which is good for most applications. However, if you have a very heavily used cluster, it could make sense to increase it a bit, such as to 2MB or 4MB.

SCI

Scalable Coherent Interface (SCI) is the final transport that MySQL Cluster natively supports. SCI is a cluster interconnect that is used commonly for all types of clusters (not only MySQL Cluster). The vendor that provides this hardware is called Dolphin Interconnect Solutions, Inc. (www.dolphinics.com).

According to MySQL AB's testing, SCI normally gives almost a 50% reduction in response time for network-bound queries. Of course, this depends on the queries in question, but it generally offers increased performance.

There are two ways you can use this interconnect. The first is through the previously mentioned TCP/IP transport, which involves an interface called SCI Sockets. This interface is distributed by Dolphin Interconnect Solutions and is available for Linux only. This is the preferred method for use between the MySQL server and data nodes. From a MySQL Cluster perspective, the network is just set up to use normal TCP/IP, but the SCI Sockets layer translates the TCP/IP into communication over SCI. For configuration information, see the SCI Sockets website, at www.dolphinics.com.

The second way to use SCI is through the native NDB transport designed for it, which uses the native SCI API. To make use of this, you need to compile MySQL Cluster with support for it, using the option `--with-ndb-sci`. This is the normal method to use between data nodes as it is normally faster than using SCI Sockets.

In order to use the native SCI transport, you need to set up your cluster configuration file (`config.ini`) with the connection information. For each SCI connection, you need to create a section called `[SCI]`. The required options to use under this option are described in the following sections.

NodeId1 and NodeID2

The two options `NodeId1` and `NodeID2` define which nodes are going to be involved in this connection. You need to define a new group for each set of nodes. For example, if you have four nodes that all use SCI, you need to define 1–2, 1–3, 1–4, 2–3, 2–4, and 3–4. Imagine if you have a large number of data nodes (such as eight or more): You might have quite a few sections. The actual number of sections required is the combination of the number of data nodes, taken two at a time ($_nC_2$).

Host1SciId0, Host1SciId0, Host2Sci0, and Host2Sci1

The values `Host1SciId0`, `Host1SciId0`, `Host2Sci0`, and `Host2Sci1` designate which SCI devices to use. Each node needs to have at least one device defined to tell it how to communicate. You can, however, define two devices for each node. SCI supports automatic failover if you have multiple SCI communication devices installed and configured to use. The actual ID number is set on the SCI card.

SharedBufferSize

The optional parameter `SharedBufferSize` specifies how much memory to devote on each end for using SCI. The default is 1MB, which should be good for most applications. Lowering this parameter can potentially lead to crashes or performance issues. In some cases, you might get better performance by increasing this parameter to slightly larger sizes.

The following is an example of a single entry (remember that you will quite often need more than just one):

```
[SCI]
NodeId1=5
NodeId2=7
Host1SciId0=8
Host2SciId0=16
```

Adding More Transports

It is possible to implement new transports relatively easily due to the separation of the transport layer from the logical protocol layer. Doing so requires writing C++ code. Although most people do not have to do this, it might prove advantageous in some cases. How to actually do it is beyond the scope of this book, but to get started, we would recommend that you do two things. First, you can refer to the source code in the directory called `ndb/src/common/transporter`, which is part of the MySQL source code distribution, and pay close attention to the class `Transporter` in `transporter.hpp`. Second, if you need assistance, you can ask on cluster@lists.mysql.com or through your support contract, if you have one.

6

Troubleshooting

This chapter covers the most common issues that you are likely to come across during your first attempted installation of MySQL Cluster.

What to Look for When Something Goes Wrong

There are several things to look for when something goes wrong in MySQL Cluster. The log files on each storage node are stored in DataDir, which is typically in /var/lib/mysql-cluster. The typical directory listing for such a folder on a storage node looks like this:

```
[user@storage] ls
ndb_3_error.log  ndb_3_out.log  ndb_3_trace.log.1
ndb_3_fs         ndb_3.pid      ndb_3_trace.log.next
```

For a management node the directory listing looks like this:

```
[user@mgm] ls
config.ini  ndb_1_cluster.log  ndb_1_out.log  ndb_1.pid
```

These files all take the form ndb_x_filename where x is the ID of the node (as either specified in config.ini or assigned when the node connects to the management daemon automatically).

The file that ends in out.log contains a log of the actions. Where there is .log.1 and so on, this means that the node crashed and recovered, and rather than replace the older files, the node simply creates new ones and adds a number to the end. This makes it fairly easy for you to go in and discover what caused the node to crash because the old log files are frozen in time at the time of the crash.

For example, this is what the log looks like after you start a storage node:

```
[user@storage] tail ndb_3_out.log
2005-08-31 11:43:53 [NDB] INFO     -- Angel pid: 2508 ndb pid: 2509
2005-08-31 11:43:53 [NDB] INFO     -- NDB Cluster -- DB node 3
```

```
2005-08-31 11:43:53 [NDB] INFO      -- Version 5.0.11 (beta) --
2005-08-31 11:43:53 [NDB] INFO      -- Configuration fetched at 10.0.0.1 port 1186
```

After a complete start of the cluster, the management server log contains far more information about the status of each node, and it records many other pieces of information, such as nodes missing heartbeats. You should monitor this proactively because, for example, regular missed heartbeats indicates a problem with load or networking in the cluster. If you spot such a problem early, you won't face a cluster shutdown, but if you fail to notice it until a shutdown, you have to fix the cause while your cluster is down, which is not a good idea.

MySQL Cluster Errors

You may encounter errors at any stage. The following sections describe common errors and their solutions.

NDBD Won't Connect

You may experience an error such as the following when you attempt to start ndbd:

```
[root@storage] ndbd
Unable to connect with connect string: nodeid=0,10.0.0.1:1186
```

This means one of two things:

- The management daemon (ndb_mgmd) has not been started.
- A firewall is preventing egress connections on port 1186 from the storage node to the management node or ingress egress on port 1186 on the management node from the storage node. It may also mean a firewall is preventing communication between cluster nodes on various ports around 2200. Firewall rules should allow communication between cluster nodes on all ports.

We strongly recommended that you not use a firewall with MySQL Cluster if at all possible. Cluster traffic is not secure, and you should not have it running on a public network. MySQL Cluster should always have a dedicated network for cluster traffic, and if clusters need to connect to the outside world, that connection should be made on a separate network with separate Ethernet cards and IP addresses.

Finally, you should be aware that many servers with recent motherboards have on-board dual Gigabit Ethernet. If you have only two storage nodes, you should be able to use a crossover cable with no switch between your storage nodes. This gives good performance, although you still have the problem of keeping your management server secure and keeping traffic between the storage node and management server secure.

NDBD **Won't Start**

ndbd may throw an error when starting. This may be trivial or may be a serious situation. There are several things to look out for if this happens, and common errors and solutions are listed here.

The following error means that the folder /var/lib/mysql-cluster does not exist:

```
Cannot become daemon: /var/lib/mysql-cluster/ndb_X.pid:
 open for write failed: no such file or directory
```

You need to create the folder /var/lib/mysql-cluster (or whatever you set DataDir to) and try again.

```
Error handler restarting system (unknown type: xxxxxxxxxx)
Error handler shutdown completed - exiting
```

This indicates a more serious error that requires further investigation. There are two places to look for errors. The first place to look, the DataDir on the storage node, now contains a file in the format ndb_pidXXXX_error.log, where XXXX is the process ID of the storage daemon. You need to open this, and you should get some serious hints, such as the following:

```
Type of error: error
Message: Invalid Configuration fetched from Management Server
Fault ID: 2350
Problem data: Unable to alloc node id
Object of reference: Could not alloc node id at 10.0.0.1 port 1186:
Connection done from wrong host imp 10.0.0.99.
ProgramName: ndbd
ProcessID: 2644
TraceFile: <no tracefile>
Version 5.0.11 (beta)
***EOM***
```

This shows that you have attempted to connect to the management server from the server 10.0.0.99, but that server is not in the config.ini on the management server, so it has told the node to go away (Connection done from wrong host ip 10.0.0.99).

The second place to look for errors is on the management host itself, where you find the file ndb_X_cluster.log (where X is the node ID of the management daemon, normally 1). In here, you get a lot of information as well as the errors, but the following line should appear somewhere fairly near the bottom:

```
2005-08-31 12:21:52 [MgmSrvr] WARNING  -- Allocate nodeid (0) failed.

Connection from ip 10.0.0.99.

Returned error string "Connection done from wrong host ip 10.0.0.99."
```

This example is fairly easy to track down because the logs tell you exactly what is wrong. Many errors do not give you such clear messages. Firewalls have a nasty habit of causing many people hours of grief because depending on where the firewall is, the various nodes can chuck out different messages or no message at all. Generally speaking, if you have a firewall, you should shut it down while installing the cluster and getting it to work, and then you should try starting your firewall and restarting your cluster.

If you see odd errors, the first thing to check is whether communication between the nodes and the management node is working. The best way to do this is to look in the management node's log file to see if a similar error is in there as well as in the storage node's error log. If the error is in both places, you know immediately that the communication between the storage node and the management node is working fine. If it is not in both places, you know that you are looking for communication problems between the two. If communication between the two is not working, you can check for firewalls and use `telnet ip.of.mgm. server 1186` from the storage node to try to connect. If the connection is refused, then either the management node did not start correctly, you have a networking problem between the nodes, or there is a firewall in the way on one of the nodes.

Arbitrator Decides to Shut Down a Node

When cluster nodes fail or networks connecting them fail, the nodes that make up the cluster undergo a complex set of decisions to decide what to do. Essentially, they attempt to avoid having two parts of the cluster split up and both of them continue to work, which results in a mess. Imagine taking two copies of your database, putting a copy on each of two machines for a few hours with lots of writes/updates to both machines, and then trying to merge the changes together at the end. It's a completely impossible task, so in order to keep your data consistent, the cluster must avoid such a partition. The technical name for such a mess is a "split brain" situation, where both halves of the brain get separated and although both sides are technically able to continue operating, one of them must shut down.

MySQL solves the split-brain problem by ensuring that even if the cluster is completely separated so a few nodes on one side of the partition cannot communicate with a few nodes on the other, they will not *both* continue to respond to queries; one half will be shut down. This means that MySQL might shut down nodes that are actually working fine as part of this process, and that is where the message "Arbitrator decided to shut down this node" comes from.

If you remove network cables between nodes for short periods of time, you will almost certainly discover that you can't just replace the network cable and continue on as usual. What happens is that if you unplug the network for long enough for the storage node to give up on connecting to the management node (or, more accurately, to fail to receive the critical number of heartbeats), the `ndbd` process will die.

This, however, is not split-brain because it is just one node dying. The following example helps explain the concept of split-brain and arbitration in more detail:

```
Five physical servers,
Server1: Storage node 1
Server2: Storage node 2, SQL node 1
Server3: Storage node 3
Server4: Storage node 4, SQL node 2
Server5: Management node
```

> **Note**
>
> For the sake of simplicity, we assume that Server5 is the arbitrator in the cluster, which it is unless you have specifically configured another node to take over this role or unless the management node is dead, in which case the storage nodes elect one of their own to act as arbitrator.

If we set NumberOfReplicas as 2, you should know that the four storage nodes will divide themselves up into groups of two (so you will have two node groups, each with two nodes in it):

```
Node Group 1: Storage nodes 1 and 2
Node Group 2: Storage nodes 3 and 4
```

Now, imagine that Physical Server 1 and Physical Server 2 are connected to one hub and that Physical Servers 3, 4, and 5 are connected to another hub. The two hubs are connected to a switch. Now consider the various failure options:

- **Physical Server 5 dies**—In this case, nothing happens. The cluster storage nodes elect a new arbitrator, and everything continues to work until the management daemon is restarted.

- **Physical Server 4 dies**—Storage Node 3, on Physical Server 3 and in the same node group as Storage Node 4, takes over the complete load, and the cluster continues to work. As soon as Physical Server 4 recovers, ndbd is restarted and rejoins the cluster.

- **The switch fails**—This is interesting. At the moment, there are two separate systems:

  - **SYSTEM 1**—Storage Node 1, Storage Node 2 and SQL Node 1
  - **SYSTEM 2**—Storage Node 3, Storage Node 4, Management Node 2, and SQL Node 2

Based on what you know already, you might think that both SQL nodes would continue to work; after all, both systems have a complete copy of the data and a SQL node. The first system does not have a management node, but as you know, the loss of a management node should not cause a cluster to crash.

As explained earlier in this section, however, you can imagine the problems if both SQL nodes continued accepting queries and then the switch was fixed. What would happen? You'd have a complete mess.

MySQL Cluster avoids this mess with the following logic, which each storage node goes through if it can no longer communicate with another node:

- Can I see more than 50% of the storage nodes in the cluster? If so, fine: Continue working.
- Can I see fewer than 50% of the storage nodes in the cluster? If so, not fine: Die.
- Can I see exactly 50% of the storage nodes in the cluster (as in the preceding example, where each storage node can see exactly two storage nodes, including itself, out of four). If so, can I see the arbitrator (typically, but not necessarily, the management node)? If so, fine: Continue working. Otherwise, die.

If you apply this logic to the preceding example, you can see that the first system will die because each storage node can see 50% of the storage nodes in the cluster but it cannot see the arbitrator (the management node).

This gets even more complicated if you have multiple node groups. Remember that each node group is made up of nodes with identical data on them. Therefore, if all nodes in *any* node group can see each other, network portioning is not an issue because clearly the other nodes cannot form a viable cluster without any node in that node group.

Therefore, in clusters with multiple node groups (that is, not where the number of replicas is equal to the number of nodes, such as in the basic two-node/two-replica cluster), the logic that each node follows in the event of it not being able to communicate with other nodes is as follows:

- Can I see at least one node in each node group? If not, shutdown (because I don't have access to a complete set of data).
- Can I see all nodes in any one node group? If so, stay alive; otherwise, die.
- If I can't see all nodes in any one node group but I can see at least one in each node group, then can I see the arbitrator? If so, stay alive. Otherwise, die to prevent split-brain problems.

If the cluster gets split in such a way that all nodes can still contact the arbitrator (but some cannot contact each other), the arbitrator keeps the first valid set of nodes to connect and tells the others to die. However, such a cluster will not normally be able to survive because storage nodes need to communicate with each other to complete queries.

Table Is Full

The error "Table is full" occurs if your DataMemory is set too low. Keep in mind that the default value for DataMemory is very low, so if it is not set in your config.ini, chances are that you will run out as soon as you try to import your tables.

Changing the DataMemory setting requires a restart of all storage nodes with the --initial parameter, so it is wise to set this parameter high so you do not encounter this problem.

Error 708

Error 708 means you do not have any more attribute metadata records remaining, which means you need to increase the value of MaxNoOfAttributes.

DBTUP Could Not Allocate Memory

The error "DBTUP could not allocate memory" can be caused by several things. First, it could result from your system being unable to address the amount of RAM that you have asked it to address. (Some Linux systems have a hard limit; FreeBSD has a maximum process size that can be changed by setting kern.maxdsiz=1000000000 in /boot/loader.conf.) If you have hit a hard limit, you can try running multiple storage nodes per server (see the section "Multiple Storage Nodes per Server," later in this chapter) and make sure you are running a recent version of your kernel.

The other cause of this problem occurs if you have set some configuration options far too high (for example, MaxNoOfLocalOperations=100000). This problem occurs because NDB uses a standard malloc() function and needs it to return a contiguous piece of memory for each memory area, but this can fail even if there is enough virtual memory and it can succeed even if there is not enough in some versions of Linux. If you are getting odd errors, it is best to reduce these parameters and see if that fixes the problem.

Multiple Storage Nodes per Server

You might face a problem allocating memory, getting an error such as "Memory allocation failure" or "DBTUP could not allocate memory for page," which may be due to your kernel not being able to allocate large quantities of RAM to one process. With FreeBSD, the simple solution is to add or change the following line in /boot/loader.conf:

```
kern.maxdsiz="1572864000"
```

> **Note**
>
> This is a value in bytes, so the preceding value allows 1.5GB per process; you can change this as appropriate. You should not set it to a value above the amount of your system RAM, and it is a good idea to set it a bit lower to avoid having your system swap excessively.
>
> Note that changing this paramater does not allow you to avoid the maximum amount that any 32-bit architecture can allocate (that is, just under 4GB). This parameter just allows you to allocate more of the system RAM to one individual process.

The other solution is to run multiple ndbd processes on each server, each with a smaller amount of RAM usage. To do this, you need to specify different data directories for each process, and we recommend that you specify the ID as well. You should also make sure that each node group has nodes on different machines; otherwise, you will get a warning explaining that a host failure (that is, a failure of one server) will bring down your cluster. The easiest way of setting up multiple storage nodes per physical server in config.ini is to specify your nodes in the following order (assuming that NoOfReplicas is set to 2):

```
Server 1, node 1 (will become Node Group 1)
Server 2, node 1 (will become Node Group 1)
Server 1, node 2 (will become Node Group 2)
Server 2, node 2 (will become Node Group 2)
```

> **Note**
> The reason for this order is that the cluster automatically forms the first node group out of the first NoOfReplicas nodes in the config.ini, so in this case, the first two nodes (because NoOfReplicas is set to 2) become Node Goup 1, and the final two become Node Group 2. You can experiment with modifying this config.ini to suit different values for NoOfReplicas.

For example, for a two data-node setup with two nodes with 1GB of DataMemory and 200MB of IndexMemory per process, you would use the following config.ini file:

```
[NDBD DEFAULT]
NoOfReplicas=2
DataMemory=1000MB
IndexMemory=200MB


#Other parameters such as MaxNoOfTransactions would probably
#need to be defined here for such a large cluster
#*** MGM NODE ***
[NDB_MGMD]
id=1
HostName=192.168.254.20


#*** Storage Nodes ***
#SERVER 1 - Node 1
[NDBD]
id=10
HostName=192.168.254.21
DataDir= /var/lib/mysql-cluster
#SERVER 2 - Node 1
[NDBD]
ID=11
HostName=192.168.254.22
```

```
DataDir= /var/lib/mysql-cluster2
#SERVER 1 - Node 2
[NDBD]
id=20
HostName=192.168.254.21
DataDir= /var/lib/mysql-cluster
#SERVER 2 - Node 2
[NDBD]
id=21
HostName=192.168.254.22
DataDir= /var/lib/mysql-cluster2
#*** SQL NODES ***

[MYSQLD]
Id=30
[MYSQLD]
Id=31
```

You would then run a number of commands to start the cluster.

On the management server (192.158.254.20 in the preceding example), you would run the following:

```
[root@mgm] cd /var/lib/mysql-cluster
[root@mgm] ndb_mgmd
```

On the first storage node (192.158.254.21 in the preceding example), you would run the following:

```
[root@storage1] ndbd --ndb-nodeid=10 --initial
[root@storage1] ndbd --ndb-nodeid=20 --initial
```

On the second storage node (192.158.254.22 in the preceding example), you would run the following:

```
[root@storage2] ndbd --ndb-nodeid=11 --initial
[root@storage2] ndbd --ndb-nodeid=21 --initial
```

You would then get the following output from running a SHOW command in the management client:

```
ndb_mgm> SHOW
Connected to Management Server at: 192.168.254.20:1186
Cluster Configuration
---------------------
[ndbd(NDB)]     4 node(s)
id=10   @192.168.254.21  (Version: 5.0.13, Nodegroup: 0, Master)
id=11   @192.168.254.22  (Version: 5.0.13, Nodegroup: 0)
id=20   @192.168.254.21  (Version: 5.0.13, Nodegroup: 1)
```

```
id=21    @192.168.254.22  (Version: 5.0.13, Nodegroup: 1)

[ndb_mgmd(MGM)] 1 node(s)
id=2     @192.168.254.20  (Version: 5.0.13)

[mysqld(API)]    2 node(s)
id=30    @192.168.254.22  (Version: 5.0.13)
id=31    @192.168.254.21  (Version: 5.0.13)
```

You can extend this to run very large numbers of storage nodes per server, and if you have 64-bit storage nodes and very large amounts of RAM, you can run a very large number of storage nodes per machine. Even though 64-bit servers can potentially run just one storage node each with a very large amount of RAM, you might prefer to run a larger number of processes, each addressing less RAM, to make them easier to manage and control as well as help you track down freak crashes.

Cluster Nodes Apparently Randomly Shut Down or Crash

There are undoubtedly some bugs left in the current versions of MySQL Cluster (through 5.0), and you might be unlucky enough to hit one of them. In some situations, individual nodes or the entire cluster may shut down for some reason.

We cannot possibly describe the solution to every possible crash—especially because many crashes result from bugs that are fixed in future releases—but we can give some general advice on what to do if such an event occurs:

1. Back up your DataDir on all your nodes. You might then want to delete all the files in the DataDir on some nodes as part of the recovery process. Having a backup allows you to report a bug or figure out what went wrong after the smoke clears and you have recovered.

2. If you have a full cluster shutdown, try to get one node in each node group working first. This can allow you to at least do a partial system restart and resume serving queries.

3. If you find that after running ndbd, nothing happens for a while and then it suddenly exits, make sure to look in the log files (see the earlier advice on the location of log files). You can also see what phase it gets stuck in by using <id> STATUS in the management client while it is starting. (You can find a list of what each phase does in the section "Startup Phases" in Chapter 1, "Installation.") Keep in mind that if you have a large database, it can take a very long time to actually start ndbd. A good thing to check is whether your RAM usage is increasing during startup and whether CPU and network usage are high. During different phases, you should either have a lot of CPU usage or have RAM usage steadily increasing. If neither of these things is occurring for a sustained period of time, you probably have a problem.

4. Make sure you always have a very recent backup. MySQL Cluster supports online backups (see Chapter 3, "Backup and Recovery"), so there is no excuse for not regularly backing up your cluster. This means that if for some reason you loose all your data, you simply recover config.ini from a backup (and it is always a good idea to keep config.ini on a floppy disk somewhere) and start all your storage nodes with --initial before importing the backup.

Note that recent versions of MySQL Cluster are very stable, and it is incredibly unusual to suffer the complete cluster shutdowns that were common in earlier releases of the software.

If you get odd errors, you can find help in several places:

- **The cluster mailing lists**—Visit http://lists.mysql.com/cluster/ and search for the error code or description you are getting. You might find that you are not the first person to suffer from this problem.

- **The MySQL Cluster forums**—At http://forums.mysql.com/list.php?25, run a search to see if others have experienced your error, and you may find a solution.

- **Google**—A search string such as "NDB error *<error #>*" at Google can be quite effective. Make sure you also search Google Groups. If you have an error description, enclose it in quotation marks, and you might get fewer, but better, results.

If you can't track down any other mentions of your problem or if none of the remedies you find fix your problem, you should report the problem to the cluster mailing list, at cluster@lists.mysql.com, and someone will attempt to work out what went wrong. If you have hit a bug, you will probably be surprised at how fast a developer will produce a patch.

You need to make sure to explain exactly what you have done and include your config.ini file and a copy of the exact error you are getting, as well as a list of what you have already tried. You should try to give your message a sensible subject, such as "NDB error xxx" rather than "help please"; this makes it easier for others to find your thread if they suffer the same problem or have a solution.

Common Setups

When you set up a complex system such as MySQL Cluster, you need to think about a number of architectural concepts, including topics such as load balancing with the MySQL servers themselves, designing for future scalability, and building a highly available setup. Quite commonly, you need to include additional software and integration between the different pieces of your server architecture. This chapter discusses some of the topics that are important regarding MySQL Cluster setups and suggests some commonly used possible solutions for the problems discussed.

Load Balancing and Failover

A couple of different pieces need to be load balanced and set up for failover in MySQL Cluster:

- **Automatic failover and load balancing within the data nodes**—This failover and load balancing happen automatically, totally transparently to your application. Generally, the application does not need to concern itself with this aspect of failover.

- **Load balancing and failover in front of the MySQL nodes**—You have to set up this type of load balancing manually. This is normally a fairly simple task, thanks to the nature of MySQL Cluster, compared to something such as MySQL replication. It is possible to read/write from any MySQL server, so failover is as simple as connecting to another MySQL server and resuming whatever task you were doing. Load balancing is also normally quite simple because the query load is already partially balanced (by the data nodes), so, depending on the types of queries you are doing, the MySQL servers normally have less load already.

There are many possibilities for setting up load balancing and failover for the MySQL servers ("SQL nodes"). The following sections discuss some different commonly used options and their pros and cons.

JDBC Driver Support

The official MySQL JDBC, Connector/J, supports automatic failover and basic load balancing capabilities, starting from MySQL Cluster version 3.1. The load balancing algorithm is fairly basic round-robin support that chooses the server to connect to. In the event that it cannot connect or gets disconnected from a server, it automatically chooses another server in the list and uses that to do queries. This failover results in losing only the transaction you are currently running, so you have to retry just that transaction.

To set up the JDBC driver for this type of failover, you need to do two additional things compared to a normal setup. First, in the connection URL, you need to specify a list of all the possible MySQL servers. The list of servers would look like this:

```
jdbc:mysql://mysqld1,mysqld2,mysqld3,mysqld4/dbname
```

Second, you need to add some additional parameters to the URL. (It is also possible to set them through the use of the JDBC Properties object instead of through the direct URL.) The minimum required URL parameters that you need to set are `autoReconnect=true`, `roundRobinLoadBalance=true`, and `failOverReadOnly=false`. These settings cause the JDBC driver to connect to a new server in the event that the current one fails, they cause it to choose the servers in a round-robin fashion, and finally, they allow the client to read and write to the failed over server. There is also a special configuration option you can use that sets all three of these settings. You set this bundle by using `useConfigs=clusterBase`.

You may consider some additional parameters as well, such as `queriesBeforeRetryMaster` and `secondsBeforeRetryMaster`. These settings cause the JDBC driver to attempt to reconnect to the original server after a set number of queries or based on time. This can be useful for allowing a server to automatically resume being used after it returns to service.

Your final JDBC URL might look similar to this:

```
jdbc:mysql://host1,host2/db?useConfigs=clusterBase&secondsBeforeRetryMaster=60
```

Now when a MySQL server fails, only your current transaction will be aborted. You can then catch the exception and retry the transaction. The parameters you have set cause the JDBC driver to transparently connect to a new server, and when you issue the queries for the transaction, they execute there. The JDBC driver attempts to fail back to the old server every 60 seconds until it succeeds.

The advantage of this setup is that, compared to other solutions, it is relatively easy to do and doesn't require any additional hardware or software.

The obvious big disadvantage of this setup is that it only works for Java, and not for any other programming languages. Another drawback is that it isn't the most sophisticated of load balancing systems, and it may not work adequately in some scenarios.

Round-Robin DNS

It is possible to set up a very primitive load balancing setup by using round-robin DNS. With this method, you basically set up a DNS name, which can resolve to any of the MySQL servers operating in your cluster. Then you need to set up a very short time-to-live (TTL) for the DNS requests. After that, you tell your application to connect to the hostname, and it then gets a different IP address each time you request to connect. It is possible to remove a node from the DNS setup when it goes down or when you want to remove it from service.

One big drawback of this method is that it doesn't gracefully handle node failures automatically. In the event of a sudden MySQL server failure, the DNS server continues to give out the IP address for the now-down server. You can handle this in two ways:

- Your application can try to connect and, if it fails, request a new DNS entry, and then it can attempt to connect again—repeating as necessary until it can finally connect. The drawback with this method is that it can take a while for the connection attempt to fail, and it can fail quite a few times if you have multiple MySQL servers down.
- You can have some sort of monitoring system that detects a MySQL server shutdown and removes it from the DNS setup. This requires additional software, and if you are going to go this route, you should look into the software solutions mentioned later in this chapter, in the section "Software Load Balancing Solutions," because they can do this detection and failure in a more graceful way than round-robin DNS.

A second problem with round-robin DNS is that the load balancing is fairly simple, and it is not dynamic. DNS always does a round-robin request serving, which in some cases is less than ideal. Some clients also ignore very small TTLs, so if you have only a small number of client machines, you might find that by chance, they all end up hitting the same SQL node for a period of time.

Hardware Load Balancing Solutions

It is possible to use a hardware load balancer with MySQL Cluster as a front end for the SQL nodes. Cisco products and products such as Big-IP are examples of hardware solutions to this problem. Normally, these hardware solutions are quite customizable and reliable. When using them with MySQL Cluster, you need to make sure they are set up to bind connections at the protocol session level. That means they should balance a single connection to the same server for the duration of the connection. The method for doing this setup depends entirely on the hardware solution in use. You should consult your hardware vendor if you have any problems making this binding.

The advantage of hardware solutions is that, generally, you can customize them to do most of what you want. For example, most hardware solutions can automatically detect whether the MySQL server isn't responding, and they can then remove it automatically from the possible connections and add it back again when the server comes back up. In addition, they can possibly do more sophisticated load balancing solutions than just round-robin.

Generally, the biggest drawback of a hardware solution is cost. Typically, hardware solutions run in the tens of thousands of dollars, which may be more than the cost of your entire cluster. In addition, technically, a hardware load balancer can become a single point of failure. To minimize this, you need to set up redundant hardware load balancers, which increases the cost and complexity of the solution.

Software Load Balancing Solutions

A number of software solutions can be used for load balancing. The most common products that can do this are Linux Virtual Server (LVS), Linux-HA, and products based on these (such as Ultra Monkey). There are many other solutions for other operating systems that should be adequate as well. A brief description of what these particular systems do should help provide insight into any other system that you might want to use:

- **LVS**—LVS (www.linuxvirtualserver.org) allows you to set up multiple Linux servers, all with a single virtual IP address. Behind the scenes, these servers can do load balancing. LVS can use many different algorithms, such as least connections, weighted round-robin, and many others. It allows for connections to be tied to a single real server, to ensure transactional integrity behind the scenes.

- **Linux-HA**—The Linux-HA project (www.linux-ha.com) is designed to provide a flexible high-availability framework for Linux (and other UNIX systems as well). The main piece of Linux-HA is called Heartbeat, which is a server that monitors the MySQL servers and removes them from possible connections if they suffer critical failures.

- **Ultra Monkey**—Ultra Monkey (www.ultramonkey.org) is a software solution that is designed to integrate Linux-HA and LVS into a single standalone solution, which allows for easier integration and building of fully load balanced and highly available solutions. The advantage of using software such as Ultra Monkey instead of the separate pieces is that it is easier to install, maintain, and configure a single-package solution.

There are a few big advantages to using a software solution such as these. First, all the software mentioned here is completely open source and freely available. Obviously, if you are designing a low-cost cluster, this is very attractive. Second, the software is very flexible. You can configure many different options, depending on the needs of your MySQL Cluster setup. This includes options such as load balancing algorithms, failover algorithms, rejoining algorithms, and so on.

The drawback of these software solutions is that they can be difficult to set up. While packages such as Ultra Monkey make setup easier, it is still generally more work to set up and maintain a system such as this than to use a hardware solution. Another possible drawback is that it can be more difficult to get support contracts to support these technologies. Many Linux distributions provide some support, and some commercial companies also provide support, but there is not a single source of support, as is possible with hardware solutions.

Cluster Topographies

There are many different ways to lay out cluster nodes across the physical systems. You need to consider many factors in your decision as to what is the best physical layout for your application. The following sections explain some of the benefits and drawbacks of running nodes in different places.

The Simplest Setup

The simplest setup that is possible for a highly available system is two main machines and a third system to hold the management server. On the two main systems, you run your application, a MySQL server, and a data node. These machines handle all the actual processing and execution of the queries. Figure 7.1 illustrates what this basic setup would look like.

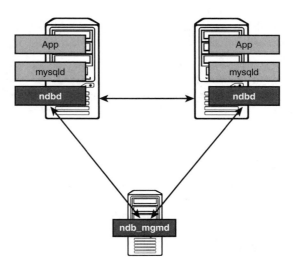

FIGURE 7.1   A basic two-machine setup.

The third machine can be relatively low performance due to the fact that it is running only the management server and does not take part in any of the query process. The only reason you need a third machine is due to network partitioning problems mentioned in previous chapters.

> **Note**
> Tim Pearson has ported the management daemon onto the OpenWRT operating system, which runs on some switches. If you have such a switch, you can use this daemon as the management daemon. See http://pcos.dyndns.org for more details.

There are a few main advantages to this setup. The most important aspect is that it doesn't require a lot of hardware, but it still maintains high availability. You can lose any one of the three machines without affecting the availability of the database. Also, the performance is relatively good because most communication can happen locally. Of course, there is network traffic between the servers, but it will be minimal compared to what it would be with more hardware.

The drawback is that this isn't a very scalable solution. It is difficult to add more machines to the environment without having to re-architect the cluster setup.

In many applications, scalability isn't as important as high availability, and this scenario is perfect for those applications. An example would be for a company intranet server for a small or medium-size business. The overall traffic in that scenario is quite small, averaging a few requests per second, but you want to maintain high availability to ensure smooth operations of the company's processes.

One thing to note is that it is possible to start with a setup such as this and then migrate to one of the larger setups mentioned later in this chapter. It might even be possible to do this migration without having to lose availability for the application. As long as you aren't growing beyond the two data nodes, it should be possible to add/move the applications and MySQL servers to different physical locations without shutting down the server.

Web Farm/MySQL Farm

As your application grows, or if you are architecting a large-scale application to begin with, you should consider some alternate architectures for your application. The following sections describe two possible setups for a more complex web application.

One-to-One Relationships

In a one-to-one relationship setup, as shown in Figure 7.2, there is a direct mapping between the MySQL server and your application server. Each instance of your application server has a single running instance of MySQL that it connects to. Normally, this is on the same physical server, using local connections between the two servers. Under this level, you can have any number of data nodes. For example, if you have four Apache servers, you would have four MySQL servers, with each of them running on the same physical server as the Apache server does, and then two data nodes running on different hardware below them. This allows for automatic load balancing because you only have to load balance in front of the application server, which is normally a relatively easy task. Also, this handles hardware failures properly because when the hardware fails, you lose both the application server and the MySQL server, which prevents any waste of resources.

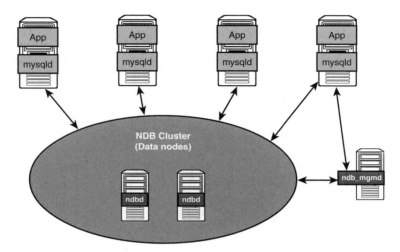

FIGURE 7.2   A one-to-one relationship.

The problem with using this method is that it doesn't work for all types of applications. It only works where you have a limited number of programs that will connect to MySQL. This works well in situations such as web applications, but it doesn't work for client/server model types of applications. In addition, it prevents you from scaling different portions of your architecture at different paces because you need to maintain the one-to-one relationship.

Creating a Separate Web Farm and MySQL Farm

In the separate farm setup, you keep the application servers separate from the entire cluster setup. This allows you to scale the different pieces of your application/database setup as needed. If you run into a bottleneck in the application, you can scale by adding more application servers, and the same could apply for MySQL servers or data nodes. As shown in Figure 7.3, these three levels of scaling can allow you to scale to even the largest workloads that applications can see.

Client/Server Applications

The client/server setup is very similar to the Web farm/MySQL farm discussed in the preceding section. The only difference is that this setup has many clients instead of a small set of application servers as the few connecting clients. An example of this would be an application that runs on a desktop client and logs directly in to MySQL across the network for reporting purposes. In this case, you will need to generally scale the MySQL servers in a much faster way, based on the number of client applications.

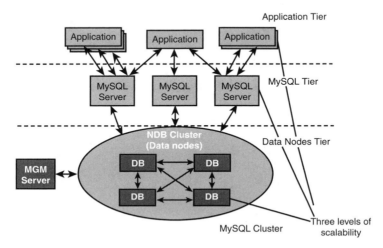

FIGURE 7.3   Scalability of multi-tier farms.

Network Redundancy

The last topic we need to discuss in order to create a highly available, scalable cluster is network redundancy. Although you can just use a normal network setup, doing so results in a single point of failure. If all your network traffic in the cluster is going across either a single router or two, and one shuts down, all the nodes disconnect and shut down your cluster. Again, there are a few different solutions for this.

The first option is to get dual-port network cards that support automatic network failover. These cards should provide automatic failover totally transparent to the cluster nodes. When purchasing these cards, you should talk to the manufacturer to ensure that you have good driver support on the operating system on which you intend to use them. With this setup, you essentially have two networks, with one network acting as the backup in case the primary fails for some reason.

A second option is to have some redundancy in the network itself. It is possible to set up a network with redundancy such that if one network component fails, others can take over the load of the failed one. In a typical setup like this, you should never have all of one node group plugged in to the same physical network device. That way, if the network device fails, you lose at most one machine from the cluster, which does not result in an entire cluster shutdown.

If you decide to go with the redundant network setup, you need to be very careful to ensure that having a larger network setup doesn't affect performance. As mentioned in Chapter 5, "Performance," network latency is extremely important, and as you add more layers of networking, it can result in an overall slowdown in cluster processing.

A

MySQL Cluster Binaries

Many binaries are included with MySQL Cluster for special uses. Many of them have been discussed in this book, but some of them have not. This appendix is designed for quick reference; you can use it to find out what a program does and get an overview of the commonly used options for the different binaries.

An Overview of Binary Options

The options for the MySQL Cluster binaries work the same as those for MySQL. They can be included in configuration files and accept short and long options in the same manner as any of the other MySQL binaries.

One option that exists for almost all the binaries discussed is called `--ndb-connectstring`, or `-c`. This option specifies to the program where to find the management server to find out the information about the structure of the cluster. Here are two examples of its use:

```
ndb_show_tables --ndb-connectstring=192.168.0.5
ndb_show_tables -c 192.168.0.5
```

To get a list of all the options that a program takes, you should run it with the `--help` or `-?` option to get output for all the possible options.

Configuration Files

The configuration file setup works the same with MySQL Cluster as with MySQL. The normal default global configuration file is `/etc/my.cnf`. In addition, a user can create a user-specific configuration file in his or her home directory as `~/.my.cnf`. This home directory configuration file is used only by the client programs and not by the server programs.

A special group is designed to be used with MySQL Cluster binaries: `[mysql_cluster]`. Any options put into this group apply to all the binaries that are involved in the cluster. The most common use of this is to specify the `ndb-connectstring` option discussed previously. The following example sets up the location of the configuration server for all cluster clients and servers that will run on the server:

```
[mysql_cluster]
ndb-connectstring=192.168.0.5
```

Individual Programs

Many different programs are used with MySQL Cluster. Some of the programs are exclusive to MySQL Cluster, whereas a lot of them are used with normal MySQL, and you may be familiar with them already. All these programs have a plethora of different command-line options that can be used with them. The following sections discuss the different programs and some of the most commonly used options.

The `mysqld` Program

`mysqld` is the normal MySQL server. It handles all the incoming client connections and handles all the SQL processing in the cluster.

The following is the most common option for `mysqld`:

Option	Description
`--ndbcluster`	Tells the MySQL server to enable the storage engine and to join the cluster setup.

The `mysql` Program

`mysql` is the default command-line client for logging in to the MySQL server. All SQL statements in this book (for example, CREATE TABLE, ALTER TABLE, SELECT) can be issued through this interface.

The following are the common options for `mysql`:

Option	Description
`--host` or `-h`	Specifies where to connect to the MySQL server.
`--user` or `-u`	Specifies which user to attempt to log in to the server as.
`--password` or `-p`	Prompts you for the password (or you can specify it on the command line). Unlike with other options, you cannot use a space between -p and *<password>* when providing it.

The ndbd **Program**

The ndbd binary represents a data node instance. You have to execute it once for each data node in the cluster setup. It is in charge of the actual physical storage and reading/writing of memory and disk with regard to the table data you manipulate.

The following are the common options for ndbd:

Option	Description
--initial	Causes **ndbd** to delete everything stored on disk. This is normally only used the first time you run the node or, in some cases, during a change of a configuration parameter.

> **Note**
> You need to be very careful.3 with the --initial option, as it can result in total data loss.

--nostart or –n	Causes **ndbd** to connect to the management server and retrieve the configuration information but not actually perform any data manipulations. It can later be fully started from within the management server, using the START option.

The ndb_mgmd **Program**

The ndb_mgmd binary represents the management server. This program reads in the cluster configuration file (config.ini) and then sends the configuration to any of the later starting nodes. It is also used for management (for example, restarting nodes, starting backups) and monitoring the health of the cluster. It also creates the cluster log, which is a central location for all cluster activities to be logged to.

The following is the most common option for ndb_mgmd:

Option	Description
--config-file or -f	Tells the management node where to find the cluster configuration. If you do not specify a file, MySQL Cluster looks for a file called config.ini in the current working directory.

The ndb_mgm **Program**

The ndb_mgm binary is the management client. It is used to log in to the management server and issue the commands to actually do the monitoring and management tasks. Normally, it runs in interactive mode, allowing you to issue commands and see their results immediately.

The following is the most common option for ndb_mgm:

Option	Description
--execute or -e	Causes the client to issue a single command and return the result instead of running in interactive mode. This option is commonly used during shell scripting for various tasks.

The ndb_desc Program

The ndb_desc program allows you to connect directly to the cluster and examine the structure of a table. This can be useful for ensuring that the cluster has the table structure you expect.

The following is the most common option for ndb_desc:

Option	Description
--database or -d	Tells the cluster what database the table is in. This option always has to be specified.

The following is an example of the ndb_desc program:

```
ndb_desc --database dbname tblname
```

The ndb_restore Program

The ndb_restore binary is used to restore a backup taken from the hot online native backup command in MySQL Cluster. It is run as many times as there are nodes in the cluster in the backup process. Chapter 3, "Backup and Recovery," provides more information.

The following are the common options for ndb_restore:

Option	Description
--backupid or -b	Specifies which backup you want to restore. Every backup is assigned an ID when it is taken, and you need to specify the ID here.
--nodeid or -n	Specifies the original node ID. Note that the node ID is stored in the backup filenames, so you can look it up if you forget it.
--restore_meta or -m	Causes the ndb_restore program to re-create all the table and index structures into the cluster. This is used only for the data you are restoring for the first node.
--restore_data or -r	Causes the ndb_restore program to re-insert the data into the cluster. This option needs to be used for all the original data nodes.

The `ndb_show_tables` Program

The `ndb_show_tables` program connects directly to the cluster (not using the MySQL server) and retrieves and outputs a list of all the tables that exist. It is most commonly used for testing that a cluster is up and has in it all the tables that should be there.

The `ndb_waiter` Program

The `ndb_waiter` program is designed to allow you to wait until the cluster has entered a certain state before returning. This can be useful when you want to take a certain action when the nodes all reach some point. The two most common times are for all of them to be started and handling requests or for them to be running but waiting to be actually started (due to the `--nostart` option for `ndbd`). The default is for `ndb_waiter` to wait until all the nodes are running.

The following is the most common option for `ndb_waiter`:

Option	Description
`--not-started`	Changes the behavior and makes the program wait until all the nodes are started but not running yet (`--nostart` option for `ndbd`).

The `perror` Program

The `perror` program is designed to aid in debugging error codes back to plain text. It accepts both MySQL and NDB error codes. The default is to look for the MySQL error code.

The following is the most common option for `perror`:

Option	Description
`--ndb`	Causes `perror` to attempt to look up the code that NDB has given.

B

Management Commands

You use the management console to communicate with the management daemon, which controls a cluster from the center. You can access the management console from any PC via the binary ndb_mgm, and then ndb_mgm can either pick up its connect string from my.cnf or you can specify it directly (see Appendix A, "MySQL Cluster Binaries"). The management daemon, ndb_mgmd, must be running on the management server in order for any commands issued to the client to take effect (otherwise, you get an error).

Displaying the Status of the Cluster/Controlling Nodes

You will make regular use of several commands to see the status of a cluster, to stop and start nodes, and to check on the memory usage of cluster nodes. The following sections cover them in detail.

The SHOW Command

The SHOW command shows you the current status of each node in the cluster, and if the node is connected, this command shows what version it is and so on. This is the quickest way of establishing how healthy your cluster is, and it is exceptionally useful when troubleshooting. For example, the following example tells you that you have two storage nodes starting, one management node already connected, and no SQL (sometimes referred to as "API" in the management console) nodes connected:

```
ndb_mgm> SHOW
Cluster Configuration
 [ndbd(NDB)]     2 node(s)
id=2    @192.168.254.13  (Version: 5.0.10, starting, Nodegroup: 0, Master)
id=3    @192.168.254.11  (Version: 5.0.10, starting, Nodegroup: 0)
[ndb_mgmd(MGM)] 1 node(s)
```

```
id=1     @192.168.254.12   (Version: 5.0.10)
[mysqld(API)]   5 node(s)
id=4 (not connected, accepting connect from any host)
id=5 (not connected, accepting connect from any host)
```

The *<id>* START, STOP, and RESTART Commands

The *<id>* START command starts nodes that already have the ndbd (storage node daemon) running and listening. Normally, when you run ndbd, it attempts to connect to the management node immediately, and it exits with an error if it cannot connect. If you start it with the -n ("no start") flag, it starts but waits for the management client to ask it to start.

So, if you run ndbd -n on Storage Node 3, the management client reports the following when asked to show the current status:

```
id=3     @192.168.254.11   (Version: 5.0.10, not started)
```

You can then start the node by issuing 3 START.

> **Note**
>
> The management client only reports "Database node 3 is being started." You should verify that the node actually does start because the client does not hang around to tell you if the node startup fails.

The *<id>* STOP command stops a storage node (the ndbd process exits). The *<id>* RESTART command restarts a storage node (without the --initial parameter).

The *<id>* STATUS Command

The *<id>* STATUS command gives you information on the current status of a node. For example, during the startup phase, it gives you the state:

```
ndb_mgm> 2 STATUS
Node 2: starting (Phase 2) (Version x.x.x)
```

Note that you can issue the command ALL instead of an ID number to get the status of all nodes (that is, ALL STATUS). This is particularly useful for detecting when nodes are in and out of single-user mode. (See the section "The ENTER SINGLE USER MODE *<sql-node-id>* Command" later in this appendix.)

The *<id>* DUMP 1000 Command

The *<id>* DUMP 1000 command causes the specified data nodes to send information to the management server about the current usage and availability of IndexMemory and DataMemory. The management node then outputs that information into the cluster log, where you can view it. This command is planned to be deprecated and replaced with a more efficient way of viewing the data in a later version of MySQL Cluster. You should never use any number other than 1000 with DUMP as doing so can lead to unwanted results.

This command is odd because it does not return the data to the management client for printing onscreen, as most other commands do. Instead, it initiates a process (which may take some time with large clusters) that records this information and then stores it in the cluster log on the management node:

```
ndb_mgm> ALL DUMP 1000
Sending dump signal with data:
0x000003e8 Sending dump signal with data:
0x000003e8
```

When you have completed the command, the cluster log contains information such as the following, where the first number is the percentage of use, and the numbers in parentheses specify the exact usage:

```
2005-08-22 18:22:11 [MgmSrvr] INFO     -- Node 2: \
     Data usage is 2(59 32K pages of total 2560)
2005-08-22 18:22:11 [MgmSrvr] INFO     -- Node 2: \
      Index usage is 1(42 8K pages of total 2336)
2005-08-22 18:22:12 [MgmSrvr] INFO     -- Node 3: \
     Data usage is 2(59 32K pages of total 2560)
2005-08-22 18:22:12 [MgmSrvr] INFO     -- Node 3: \
      Index usage is 1(42 8K pages of total 2336)
```

Logging Commands

The logging flexibility of MySQL Cluster is enormous. The following sections cover the commands you can use to log precisely what you want to log and where.

The CLUSTERLOG ON and CLUSTERLOG OFF Commands

The CLUSTERLOG commands enable and disable cluster logging. You can pass a severity level to these command, but we suggest that you use the CLUSTERLOG FILTER command (see the section "The CLUSTERLOG FILTER <severity> Command," later in this appendix) to do that.

This command should make it clear that it has worked:

```
ndb_mgm> CLUSTERLOG ON
Cluster logging is enabled
```

The CLUSTERLOG TOGGLE Command

The CLUSTERLOG TOGGLE command toggles the cluster log (that is, it inverts the current setting, so if it is currently enabled, TOGGLE disables it and vice versa). It also tells you whether cluster logging is enabled or disabled after you have issued the command, as CLUSTERLOG ON and CLUSTERLOG OFF do, as in the following example:

```
ndb_mgm> CLUSTERLOG TOGGLE;
        Cluster logging is enabled.
```

```
ndb_mgm> CLUSTERLOG TOGGLE;
        Cluster logging is disabled
```

The CLUSTERLOG INFO Command

The CLUSTERLOG INFO command prints information about the current cluster logging status, telling you what severities (see Table B.1 in the following section) are currently being logged globally:

```
ndb_mgm> CLUSTERLOG INFO
Severities enabled: INFO WARNING ERROR CRITICAL ALERT
```

The CLUSTERLOG FILTER *<severity>* Command

The CLUSTERLOG FILTER *<severity>* command enables or disables logging of each severity level. If a severity level is turned on, all events with a priority less than or equal to the category thresholds are logged. You set the thresholds for each category individually for each node or globally by using the CLUSTERLOG command, which is covered shortly. If the severity level is turned off, no events belonging to that severity level are logged. This is a global setting (that is, it affects all nodes in the cluster).

The severity levels shown in Table B.1 are used in MySQL Cluster.

TABLE B.1   MySQL Cluster Severity Levels

Level Number	Level Name	Description
1	ALERT	A condition that should be corrected immediately, such as a corrupted system database
2	CRITICAL	Critical conditions, such as device errors or insufficient resources
3	ERROR	Conditions that should be corrected, such as configuration errors
4	WARNING	Conditions that are not errors but that might require handling
5	INFO	Informational messages, which may be useful for troubleshooting before you submit a bug report or a request for help
6	DEBUG	Debugging messages, which you almost certainly want to ignore

Calling CLUSTERLOG FILTER simply inverts the current selection, so issuing CLUSTERLOG FILTER ALERT twice when the filter starts off enabled results in disabling and then enabling logging (remember that you can see which severity levels are currently being logged with the command CLUSTERLOG INFO):

```
ndb_mgm> CLUSTERLOG FILTER ALERT
ALERT disabled
ndb_mgm> CLUSTERLOG FILTER ALERT
ALERT enabled
```

The *<id>* CLUSTERLOG *<category>=<threshold level>* Command

The *<id>* CLUSTERLOG *<category>=<threshold level>* command initiates logging of *<category>* events with priority less than or equal to *<threshold>* in the cluster log. Note that this can be set globally (do not specify an *<id>* field) or for each node individually (specify *<id>*). Note that the severity level must be enabled for any logging to take place; if you have disabled filtering for all CRITICAL errors, there will be no messages that belong to the CRITICAL severity level in your log file, regardless of what you set with the CLUSTERLOG command. You can check what severity levels are currently enabled by using the CLUSTERLOG INFO command.

For example, by using this command, you can set a threshold of 7 for STARTUP events, but a threshold of 2 for BACKUP events. In this way, you can log what you want to log as much as you like, while reducing the amount of junk in the log files. You can also set different log levels for each node. This has clear uses; for example, when trying to track down a connection error on one node, you can get an enormous amount of information logged that is all relevant to that particular node's connection errors but not accumulate enormous quantities of irrelevant logging information from other nodes that are functioning fine.

You can use the following categories:

```
STARTUP (default: 7)
SHUTDOWN (default: 7)
STATISTICS (default: 7)
CHECKPOINT (default: 7)
NODERESTART (default: 7)
CONNECTION (default: 7)
INFO (default: 7)
ERROR (default: 15)
CONGESTION
DEBUG
BACKUP
```

The threshold level is a number between 0 and 15, where 0 is the most important events, and 15 is purely for information and debugging. Each level also includes the lower levels as well. For example, if you specify a threshold of 4, it automatically includes 3, 2, 1, and 0.

For example, to log events with a threshold level (importance) of less than or equal to 5 from connections involving Node 2, you would enter this:

```
ndb_mgm> 2 CLUSTERLOG CONNECTION=5
Executing CLUSTERLOG CONNECTION=5 on node 2 OK!
```

Miscellaneous Commands

The following sections cover some other commands that you may find useful.

The ENTER SINGLE USER MODE <sql-node-id> Command

Single-user mode allows you to restrict database system access to a single SQL node. When you enter single-user mode, all connections to all other SQL nodes are closed gracefully, and all running transactions are aborted. No new transactions are allowed to be started.

Entering single-user mode is pretty straightforward:

```
ndb_mgm> ENTER SINGLE USER MODE 4
Entering single user mode
Access will be granted for API node 4 only.
Use ALL STATUS to see when single user mode has been entered.
```

When the cluster has entered single-user mode, only the designated SQL node is granted access to the database. You can use the ALL STATUS command to see when the cluster has entered single-user mode:

```
ndb_mgm> ALL STATUS
Node 2: single user mode (Version 5.0.10)
Node 3: single user mode (Version 5.0.10)
```

This shows you when the storage nodes have switched over to single-user mode. So in this example, the storage nodes have IDs of 2 and 3.

The EXIT SINGLE USER MODE Command

The EXIT SINGLE USER MODE command returns to normal mode. SQL nodes waiting for a connection (that is, for the cluster to become ready and available) are then allowed to connect. The MySQL server denoted as the single-user SQL node continues to run (if it is connected) during and after the change.

The SHUTDOWN Command

The SHUTDOWN command shuts down all nodes in the cluster, including the management daemon and all storage nodes. Note that it does not actually stop SQL nodes (MySQL servers), but it does remove their ability to do anything to tables in the cluster. Note that you cannot run this command when in single-user mode.

Running this command is fairly straightforward:

```
ndb_mgm> shutdown
2 NDB Cluster storage node(s) have shutdown.
NDB Cluster management server shutdown.
```

The PURGE STALE SESSIONS Command

The PURGE STALE SESSIONS command is used in some older versions of MySQL Cluster to fix a bug. It resets reserved node IDs that should be reset each time a node shuts down but sometimes are not. Normally, this command returns "No sessions purged." If you have problems connecting a node, with errors implying that it is already connected, you can try this command to see if it fixes the problem. This command is not dangerous and will not cause your cluster any damage; the worst-case scenario is that it may do nothing at all. Typically, it will return the following output, which means that it has done nothing:

```
ndb_mgm> PURGE STALE SESSIONS;
No sessions purged
```

The START BACKUP Command

The START BACKUP command causes MySQL Cluster to begin making a backup. You can use an optional parameter with START BACKUP to determine what action to take after starting the backup. The three possible options are NOWAIT, WAIT STARTED, and WAIT COMPLETED. If you do not specify a level, the default is WAIT COMPLETED. If you specify the NOWAIT option, the START BACKUP command returns immediately, while the request is sent to the management daemon to start the backup. WAIT STARTED causes the command to return after all the data nodes acknowledge the command to begin the backup. Finally, WAIT COMPLETED returns only after all the data nodes have confirmed that the backup completed successfully.

In most cases, you will want to use WAIT COMPLETED, which tells you when the backup completes:

```
ndb_mgm> START BACKUP WAIT COMPLETED
Waiting for completed, this may take several minutes
Node 2: Backup 6 started from node 1
Node 2: Backup 6 started from node 1 completed
 StartGCP: 1580 StopGCP: 1583
 #Records: 4098 #LogRecords: 0
 Data: 65688 bytes Log: 0 bytes
```

The ABORT BACKUP <backup id> Command

The ABORT BACKUP <backup id> command causes the nodes to interrupt the backup in progress. It is not possible to resume after the abort, and a new START BACKUP is required to begin a new backup process. You can use ABORT BACKUP on backup IDs that are not in progress without getting any errors. If you successfully abort a backup, you get a message confirming that it was successful. For example, to abort backup ID 10, you would use the following command:

```
ndb_mgm> ABORT BACKUP 10
Abort of backup 10 ordered
Node 2: Backup 10 started from 1 has been aborted. Error: 1321
```

C

Glossary of Cluster Terminology

This book uses a lot of special terminology in reference to MySQL Cluster. This appendix is designed to be a quick reference of what a term means with regard to MySQL Cluster. Each term is defined briefly.

arbitration   Arbitration is the process by which MySQL Cluster prevents a split-brain scenario from occurring. In the event of network failures such that there are possibly two survivable clusters that do not communicate, arbitration is used to decide which set of nodes is allowed to continue running. The arbitrator is the node that is in charge of making this decision.

arbitrator   The arbitrator is the node that is in charge of deciding which set of nodes will remain running in the event of a network partitioning scenario. This is normally the management node, but it can also be an SQL node if you manually set ArbitrationRank to 1 or 2 for the SQL node(s). In the event that the arbitrator fails, a new node is automatically elected as the new arbitrator.

checkpoint   Checkpointing is the process by which MySQL Cluster writes data and logs from memory onto disk. There are two different types of checkpoints: local and global. In a local checkpoint, all the data is written from memory to disk. In a global checkpoint process, the REDO log is written to disk.

cluster log   The cluster log is a centralized log that is generated by the management node reporting on various actions taken by the cluster and its member nodes. This includes actions such as a node failure, a node restart, arbitration, backups, and many other cluster actions. In addition to the cluster log, there are node logs, which are generated locally for each individual node on the disk local to the node.

data node   A data node is a node in MySQL Cluster that stores all the actual data. Normally, all access to the data is done through SQL nodes, not directly to the data node. The data nodes are also in charge of executing any parts of the query that are passed down to them from the SQL nodes.

fragment   Data in MySQL Cluster is horizontally partitioned into pieces that are spread around the different data nodes. These pieces are called *fragments* of data. There is a number of fragments equal to the number of data nodes in the MySQL Cluster setup, each one being approximately $1/N$ of the data, where N is the number of data nodes. For example, if you have 4 data nodes, each fragment is approximately 1/4 of the data.

hash index   MySQL Cluster uses a hash index to implement both primary and unique keys. Rather than reference the data directly, MySQL Cluster instead produces a hash of the data and references the generated hash directly. An example of the hash used in MySQL Cluster is MD5 (for Message Digest 5).

InnoDB   InnoDB is one of the standard transactional engines in MySQL. InnoDB makes use of the normal transactional concepts of REDO and UNDO logs in order to maintain transactional consistency. InnoDB is not clustered, but it can be used along with cluster tables on a single system.

management client   ndb_mgm is the management client, which provides an interface to the management daemon, which runs on the management node. The management client can be run on any machine that has unfirewalled access to the management daemon.

management node   The management node is used for both configuration and control of MySQL Cluster. It is a central repository for the configuration information that all other nodes communicate with to find out the MySQL Cluster setup. In addition, it is used for management purposes, such as centralized logging, starting and monitoring of backups, monitoring of node status, and shutting down of nodes in the cluster.

The management node is not required to be running for normal operations, but in most cases, you want it to always be running for the previously described management purposes. It is possible to set up multiple management servers for redundancy purposes. In such a case, one is the active node, and the second node serves as the backup in the event that the primary is unable to be contacted.

master node   In every MySQL Cluster setup, one node is designated as the master node. This is done automatically, based on which data node has been running the longest. The master designation is used only internally for many different processes, such as global checkpointing and node recovery. In the event that the master node fails, the surviving nodes automatically elect another node as the master.

MyISAM   MyISAM is a nontransactional stored engine that exists in MySQL. In it, data is stored in a normal disk-based setup; it is not clustered. MyISAM must currently be used for the system tables.

network partitioning   Network partitioning can occur in a cluster that gets separated and leaves behind two possible survivable pieces. A set of nodes is considered able to survive if it contains at least one node from each node group in the cluster. For example, if there are four data nodes and they get split into two groups of two from different node groups, this would be a possible network partitioning situation. This situation is also called a "split brain" problem. To prevent this from occurring, MySQL Cluster uses a process called arbitration.

node   A node is a single running instance of software in MySQL Cluster. There are three different types of nodes: data, SQL, and management nodes. A single physical computer may run single or multiple nodes.

node group   A node group is a set of data nodes that all contain the same data. This designation is important for knowing whether a cluster can survive a node failure. As long as there is at least one node running from each node group, the cluster is able to continue running and processing requests. Each node group has in it a number of data nodes equal to the value of NoOfReplicas. There is a number of node groups equal to the number of data nodes divided by NoOfReplicas.

partitioning   Data in MySQL Cluster is horizontally partitioned. This means that a single table has different rows stored on different data nodes. Partitioning means that no single node normally has all the data (except with small clusters, where the NoOfReplicas is equal to the number of data nodes). Currently, data is always partitioned according to a MD5 hash of PRIMARY KEY. MySQL 5.1 adds the ability to manually control this, which can possibly lead to more efficient storage, improved querying, and better performance.

replica   A replica is considered a copy of data. If you have two replicas of your data, you have two complete copies of the data across your cluster. You can control how

many copies to keep by using the NoOfReplicas setting. Technically, you can set NoOfReplicas from 1 to 4, with 2 being the most common setting.

SCI (scalable coherent interface)   SCI is a clustering interconnect that can be used in place of normal TCP/IP in MySQL Cluster. Generally, SCI has lower latency and much better performance than TCP/IP-based connections, but it costs more for the hardware compared to traditional TCP/IP interconnects.

shared-nothing clustering   MySQL Cluster uses shared-nothing clustering, which means that each physical server in the cluster setup is a completely separate system from the other physical servers. All disks, RAM, CPUs, and so on are completely independent from each other in this setup. This is in contrast to shared-disk clustering, in which there is a single storage subsystem that all the nodes use.

split-brain   Split-brain is a concept in which a cluster of machines gets a network-partitioned scenario, and two separate clusters can continue to process requests. This is a very dangerous situation and is prevented by arbitration.

SQL node   An SQL node is a normal MySQL server (which must have MySQL-Max installed or be compiled with the option --with-ndbcluster) that has been set up to connect and communicate with a cluster setup. You interface to this by using any of the normal MySQL clients and APIs.

synchronous replication   Replication in MySQL Cluster is automatically done in a transparent, synchronous fashion. This means that when you are writing data to the cluster, the data is copied to multiple places by the time your query returns. It is guaranteed to already exist in multiple places. This is how the MySQL Cluster setup can do transparent failover because there is more than one copy of the data across the data nodes. In the event that the cluster cannot successfully replicate the data, the transaction is aborted. See also *two-phase commit*.

T-tree index   A T-tree index in MySQL Cluster is the normal, ordered index that exists for tables. This is similar in structure to a B-tree index that is used for InnoDB and MyISAM, but it is optimized for access in main memory systems. It can be used to resolve all the same queries that a B-tree index can resolve.

two-phase commit   Two-phase commit is the mechanism that MySQL Cluster uses in order to be able to guarantee that synchronous replication is taking place. This happens automatically, based on the NoOfReplicas setting. Two-phase commit is sometimes abbreviated as 2PC.

Index

D

J – K – L

M

RAM (Random Access Memory)
allocation failure errors, 157
automatic calculating of requirements, 60
constraint requirements, 58
DataMemory parameter. *See DataMemory*
DBTUP errors, 157
field width reduction, 62
index requirements, 57
IndexMemory parameter. *See IndexMemory*
LockPagesInMainMemory setting, 83
NDB requirements, 55
normalizing databases, effect of, 61-62
page storage system, 58
primary key requirements, 57
replica requirements, 58
requirements for installation, 22
requirements overview, 55-56
row overhead, 57
storage node requirements, 23
table requirements, calculating, 56-60
recovery, SQL nodes issues, 95. *See also* **failures**
REDO
logs, 44
NoOfFragmentLogFiles settings, 80-81
RedoDataBuffer setting, 89
redundant networks, 170-171
replicas of data
memory required by, 23
NoOfReplicas setting, 35, 73-74
RAM requirements, 58
response time, 129-130, 145
restarts
backups with, 68
config.ini changes with, 67
RESTART command, 180
restarting clusters, 44-46
restarting MySQL, 40
rolling clusters, 121-124
restoring backups
--backupid ndb_restore option, 176
ID specification, 104
mysqld sections for, 104
mysqldump for, 106-107
ndb_restore program for, 104-106
--nodeid ndb_restore option, 176
options for ndb_restore, 104
parallel restores, 106-107
--restore_data ndb_restore option, 176
--restore_meta ndb_restore option, 176

single-user mode for, 103
speeding up, 106-107
result sets, 136
rolling cluster restarts, 121-124
root passwords, 118
round-robin DNS, 165
rows
creating, 41-42
overhead size, 57
width limitations, 22
RPM binaries, 24, 28-29

S

scalability
defined, 129
network I/O, 130
network redundancy, 170-171
one-to-one server relationships, 169
separate Web and MySQL farms, 169
simplest setup, from, 168
Scalable cluster interconnect (SCI), 147-149
scans
MaxScanBatchSize setting, 94
parameters of config.ini, 79-80
SCI (Scalable cluster interconnect), 147-149
scripts
all SQL nodes, issuing commands to, 125
example, 120
rolling cluster restarts, 121-124
security issues, 118
timed execution of, 120
security
APF firewalls, 115-117
application servers, 111
application user, isolation from, 114
chrooted environments, 125-128
firewalls recommended, 109, 111
firewalls, software, 114-117
forwarding, disallowing, 111
IP address issues, 111
management daemon access, 109
network design, 109, 111
network traffic control overview, 109
overview of, 109-110
partitioning of network, 111
permissions tables, 118
ports, number required, 109
privilege level of MySQL, 117-118
root passwords, 118
script sockets, 118
skip-networking option, 118